Developing Authorship and Copyright Ownership Policies

Developing Authorship and Copyright Ownership Policies

Best Practices

Allyson Mower

ROWMAN & LITTLEFIELD
Lanham • Boulder • New York • London

Published by Rowman & Littlefield
An imprint of The Rowman & Littlefield Publishing Group, Inc.
4501 Forbes Boulevard, Suite 200, Lanham, Maryland 20706
www.rowman.com

86-90 Paul Street, London EC2A 4NE

British Library Cataloguing in Publication Information Available

Library of Congress Cataloging-in-Publication Data

Names: Mower, Allyson, author.
Title: Developing authorship and copyright ownership policies : best practices / Allyson Mower.
Description: Lanham : Rowman & Littlefield, 2024. | Includes bibliographical references and index.
Identifiers: LCCN 2023044613 (print) | LCCN 2023044614 (ebook) | ISBN 9781538173848 (cloth) | ISBN 9781538173855 (paperback) | ISBN 9781538173862 (ebook)
Subjects: LCSH: Copyright—United States. | Authors and publishers—United States. | Fair use (Copyright)—United States. | Universities and colleges—Law and legislation—United States.
Classification: LCC KF3020 .M69 2024 (print) | LCC KF3020 (ebook) | DDC 346.7304/82—dc23/eng/20231002
LC record available at https://lccn.loc.gov/2023044613
LC ebook record available at https://lccn.loc.gov/2023044614

Contents

Preface

The term "authorship" in recent years has come to be comprised of complex layers of meaning: Is authorship a reward, should it be a way to honor someone, can we confer it on machines? The basic question has essentially become: Who gets to be an author? This book provides potential answers by looking closely at how the U.S. Copyright Act defines authorship and, in turn, how institutional copyright ownership and authorship policies provide more detailed terms and conditions.

Developing Authorship and Copyright Ownership Policies: Best Practices discusses the concept of authorship, but it remains primarily practical and provides clarity for the purpose of accurately determining authorship. In writing the book, I aspire to achieve equity and inclusion within the scholarly communication system. In the last fifteen years of serving as a scholarly communication and copyright librarian, I have observed how the complex layers that have come to surround authorship have led to harmful and unjust practices, such as not including legitimate authors or making the process of becoming an author seem impossible and confusing. In my opinion, these types of actions remain unnecessary within the scholarly research enterprise given how many simple and easy-to-implement solutions exist, the first being a basic understanding of copyright ownership.

The overview of copyright ownership will be brief so you will not feel required to become an expert in order to know how authorship works. You will learn just enough to know how to manage your own authorship as well as others' as you work in or with groups and teams.

Chapter 1 discusses the various concepts behind the term "authorship" to help illuminate copyright ownership in chapter 2. The two ideas—authorship and copyright ownership—get combined in chapter 3 to demonstrate how they work together within the scholarly communication system. Chapters 4 and 5 move into discussion of best practices in policy development with a focus on equity, diversity, and inclusion. Chapters 6 and 7 provide several sample policies from a range of institutions. Chapter 6 focuses on copyright ownership policies and chapter 7 highlights authorship policies.

It takes some thought and careful attention to accurately prepare an authorship policy or plan and put it into practice, especially for large, diverse, or dispersed research groups, but as members of the scholarly communication system—be it an academic author, a research administrator, an editor, a librarian, or publishing staff member—it is possible to ensure equitable author-ship opportunities and experiences.

How you build and manage a research team will impact how authorship plays out in the various reports, websites, books, presentations, infographics, articles, and other products and works of authorship that get created. This book, however, does not address how to build a diverse research team. It points out issues surrounding lack of racial and gender diversity within the historical context of academic authorship, but does not provide a how-to for ethical team building. Please consult the resources and further reading section for good references on that topic. What this book does provide are useful tips on how to interpret and write a policy that holistically incorporates all aspects of copyright ownership and how copyright ownership impacts the process of authorship.

Acknowledgments

To an excellent editor, Charles Harmon, who encouraged this book and made it better. To my spouse, Alyssa Williams, for the endless support. To all the institutions who gave permission for their policies to be included: Association for Computing Machinery, Coalition for Diversity & Inclusion in Scholarly Communication, Springer-Nature, University of Chicago Press, University of Texas System, University of Toledo, University of Utah. And to all the academic authors, especially any who may have experienced being unfairly left off of a work of authorship.

1

Concepts of Authorship

The ability to act as an academic author has depended on the foundational institutions and the broader social and legal realities in America. In 1876, the first systematic, concerted effort to conduct research and advance knowledge emerged at Johns Hopkins University through an emphasis on professors developing programs of graduate studies.[1] The general expectations focused on incorporating original, independent research into the curriculum. But this came after a long line of various "firsts" in American history related to research, higher education, and academic authorship. As table 1.1 shows, the foundational approaches emerged from predominantly White male institutions. White women, and Black, Indigenous, and People of Color (BIPOC) wrote and produced works, but—as table 1.2 shows—that happened at a much later date in the chronology of academic authorship.

The first women's college and first Black college did not open until 1837.[2] The first Indigenous college was founded in 1968.[3] The Association for the Advancement of Women, while not strictly a scholarly society, was established in 1873 and BIPOC scholarly societies in America were organized at various time points from 1842 to 1966:[4]

1842 American Oriental Society
1904 Hispanic Society of America
1915 Association for the Study of Negro Life and History[5]
1966 Middle East Studies Association of North America
1969 Association for Jewish Studies

Scholarly presses started by women and BIPOC also have their own history. Howard University Press began in 1972 and Dine College Press was launched in the 1970s as the college was being organized.[6] These facts become relevant because they set a foundation for later chapters in this book focused on the importance of equity, diversity, and inclusion (EDI) in authorship policies

Table 1.1. A Chronological Timeline of Academic Authorship at Predominately White Male Institutions in the United States Developed by the Author for an Institutional Bibliography Found at https://authors.lib.utah.edu

First college	Puritan's College (now called Harvard) (1636)
First scholarly society	American Philosophical Society (1743)
First scholarly journal	*Transactions of the American Philosophical Society* (1771)
First legislation to promote research and creativity	U.S. Constitution, Section 8 (1787) and Copyright Act (1790)
First federal government effort to fund research	Smithsonian (1846), National Academy of Sciences (1863)
First press at a college/university	Cornell University Press (1869)
First employment expectation to conduct research and advance knowledge	Johns Hopkins University (1879)
First federal government effort to promote application of research to military, agriculture, engineering	National Research Council (1916)
First federal effort to fund art	National Endowment for the Arts (1965)
First federal effort to fund humanities	National Endowment for the Humanities (1965)

Table 1.2. A Timeline Showing Equity, Diversity, and Inclusion Firsts at Predominantly White Male Institutions

Puritan's College (aka Harvard)	Black faculty member (1870)
	Female faculty member (1919)
American Philosophical Society and Transactions of the American Philosophical Society	Elected an American woman (1869)
	Published a female author (1935)
	Elected a Black American (1950)
	Published a BIPOC author (unknown)
Johns Hopkins University	Female faculty member (1924)
	Black faculty member (1960)

at academic institutions, scholarly societies, journals, presses, and other scholarly communication venues.

As these tables and list demonstrate, academic authorship has a particular definition and history within the United States. This chapter introduces the concepts prevalent in academic authorship based on these historical details along with evidence from cross-disciplinary literature as well as employment statements regarding retention, promotion, and tenure (RPT) of faculty which help inform authors themselves in their role as research managers.[7] The concepts covered in this chapter (and this book overall) also hope to inform professionals who work within the scholarly communication system, such as research and academic administrators, publishers, editors, and librarians. Academic authors work within complex institutions and conduct research for a range of purposes that might differ from other types of authors. As this chapter will show, uncovering the structures of motivation that exist within employment expectations of an institution helps delineate the fundamental components of authorship within the domain of scholarly communications.

For purposes of this book, I argue that academic authorship consists of three components—author-as-employee, scholarly critique of an original expression, and academic/research institution–as–motivating structure—and each receives distinct treatment in this chapter. The components also get considered as a whole in order to fully inform how authorship relates to scholarly communication. Additional concepts of academic authorship include individuality, originality, teaching-research dichotomy within knowledge advancement, readership, and audience. A newer area of academic authorship also gets explored and that concept is what I have come to call author-as-convener. The prevalence of team or group science has increased over the last two decades,[8] and while publishers and research administrators have had to adapt to this new reality, research employment expectations and internal processes and cultures have not.[9] This book hopes to bridge the gap between the scholarly and scientific community and institutional cultures.

Scholarship, as described by cultural theorist Doris Bachmann-Medick, represents one form of expression within a culture. Other forms of expression include art, theatre, rituals, and festivals. Bachmann-Medick calls scholarship "theory-forming microevents" and contends that the writing and production of scholarship has largely been ignored and "greatly underestimated."[10] Michel Foucault defines authorship as a functional mode to bring forth and circulate "certain discourses within a society,"[11] which fine arts researcher Estelle Barrett says "requires us [. . .] to focus on the forms the work takes and the institutional contexts that allow it to take such form."[12] In tracing the origins of the concept of copyright ownership and literary property, research professor Mark Rose determined that authorship represented an imprinting of an author's personality or personhood onto a work.[13]

My initial desire to approach a study of academic authorship came after reading Derek Price's *Little Science, Big Science and Beyond . . .* , where quantifiable laws, statistics, and predictions define the world of scientometrics and info-metrics.[14] In a succinct sentence near the end of the book, Price says simply that journal articles from scientific disciplines represent an expression of a scholar or group of scholars at a particular point in time. This very human-centered definition among quantifiable metrics stood out to me and I wondered if it matched what others have said about scholarly communication in other disciplines and in different contexts. I consulted literature from library and information science, fine arts, communication, philosophy, literary criticism, sociology, history of authorship and copyright, and history of higher education to inform a better understanding of academic authorship. I also conducted a study of six employment statements detailing approaches to RPT in order to determine how authorship gets defined on a discipline basis within an institution. The statements came from six different colleges at a single university representing humanities, science, fine arts, education, engineering, and social and behavioral sciences.

AUTHOR-AS-EMPLOYEE

The U.S. copyright statute defines the term "author" simply as one who is responsible for the creation of a work. The term has also come to mean a person fulfilling a particular function, as Foucault referenced. That function is to manage meaning, according to recent scholars Eva Mroczek and Damon Young.[15, 16] Writing scholar Lisa Ede provides an even more precise definition: "An author is one who struggles with and through language to create something new, a text that embodies, however imperfectly, the writer's intentions."[17] The idea of authorship, according to Ede, emerged in 1710 and represents a "complex reflection of culture."[18] Language represents one of those complexities of culture, especially as computer-based languages emerge, which I discuss in the next section. Ede's definition provides solid footing in reminding us that a human, to be an author, works through language of whatever construct to bring forth a new expression. Do these definitions apply to academics who are expected to conduct research and communicate it to others as a condition of employment? Do academic authors manage meaning? And do they create something new through an expression of language?

Academic institutions as employers expect employees categorized as faculty to spend a portion of their time investigating an area of a discipline on an individual basis, maintain that investigation during the time of employment, and describe what they find during their investigations to others in the discipline. Each of the employment statements I studied focused heavily on the expectation of originality of the author's scholarly expression arrived at through independent work and with a sustained level of investigation. All of them indicated that the expected audience of the research outcome are those within the author's discipline. None of them indicated that the general public was the expected audience. Quality of the output rose above both quantity and impact. Based on these employment expectations, I would argue that academic authors are responsible for the creation of a work by virtue of being required to conduct independent and original research. Academic authors use some form of language to express the results of the independent and original research. They also manage meaning for peers within their discipline and for students whom they teach and who work with them on their research.

A less explored, at least theoretically, aspect of academic authorship is readership and audience. For whom should academic authors create new knowledge and manage meaning: learners, academic peers, and the general public? Exploring the ethics of information access and readership as a separate inquiry could help further develop responses to this element of academic authorship, especially as the question relates to the motivating structures—in the form of RPT statements—found within academic institutions.

SCHOLARLY CRITIQUE OF AN ORIGINAL EXPRESSION

Expression, medium, and form all have close relationships. An expression represents a product of the mind: one scholar's (or a group of scholars') original communication of an idea. That expression or communication comes through a language: spoken, written, visual, programmed. The language utilized directly impacts the medium and form. Musical notation and lyrics represent a type of language. Mathematics another. Extensible and hypertext markup languages yet another. These languages can be utilized to express meaning in a wide range of media. Paper represents one type of media. Stone, clay, canvas, computer disks serve as additional examples. Descriptive prose about a scientific finding written with ink on paper in Korean embodies expression, medium, and language. Poetry typed in English using word-processing software stored on a computer hard drive and displayed on the web using hypertext markup language is yet another kind of expression, medium, language, and form.

The originality of what gets expressed will depend on the discipline in which the academic author remains active. If the expression or communication has already been made by a previous scholar, then, by definition, it would not be considered original. The academic author will have been derelict in his, her, or their scholarly duty to develop a strong understanding of what has come before through independent study. If the expression or communication has not yet been made by a previous scholar, that author will have achieved the expected originality requirement of faculty employment and will have met his, her, or their scholarly duty to understand a discipline well enough to know what expressions may not have been communicated. In turn, the academic author will cause the discipline to progress by creating new knowledge and managing meaning within the discipline. Non-academic authors and their publishers looking to sell their books also need a good understanding of what has come before for practical reasons of producing popular books and avoiding copyright infringement. The additional requirement of knowing the history, methodology, and trajectory of a discipline is unique to academic authors. This unique aspect of authorship reinforces the need to more thoroughly understand the concepts involved in academic authorship.

ACADEMIC INSTITUTION-AS-MOTIVATING STRUCTURE

An institution represents a collection of people centered around a common pursuit. The activities pursued influence the development of an institutional culture. Academic authors operate within institutions of higher learning and contribute to their culture. Higher education institutions are complex entities in the sense that faculty employees lead the institution through the management of decentralized departments, colleges, and libraries. Faculty draft discipline-level RPT statements and also craft university-wide policies.

These discipline-level employment statements and campus-wide policies define the common pursuit of the institution. Such pursuits center on the well-being of students and attending to the advancement of knowledge. The two go hand in hand. Teaching involves conveying knowledge by way of instruction while advancing a subject focuses on moving it forward by engaging in and conducting research. Teaching can be used as a powerful communication tool to advance a topic to those who may be new to the discipline, but the information is typically previously known or understood by the teacher. Advancement of knowledge necessitates investigation, close study, and familiarity with appropriate research methodologies—all of which can make one a better teacher of a subject matter. The investigation and the results need to be communicated to those actively working within the discipline and critiqued by them. Learnings from research can get communicated in a classroom setting, but if limited to the classroom, a broader audience of peers and their critique will be missed.

While the audience needs to be wider in scope than students in a classroom, the employment expectation does not typically go beyond communicating results to those active in the discipline. The term "publishing" (i.e., to make public) is a slight misnomer because the expectation, as currently conceived of within RPT statements, is not to communicate findings to the public in general, but to a limited public of academic peers as potential critics.

READERSHIP, AUDIENCE, IMPACT

The academic community most familiar with an academic author's scholarly expression defines that author's readership and audience. That same audience will also inform any notion of impact through the process of reading, testing, and judging its quality, novelty, and originality. How does an academic author find the right academic community in which to distribute his, her, or their scholarly expression for critique? And how do academic authors find evidence of the originality of their scholarly expression? This is where the teaching and research aspects of author-as-employee become important and where publishers, publisher policies, as well as librarians and library collections begin to intersect.

To discover the trajectory of a discipline, a researcher needs to learn about the discipline through extended study, which requires a curated academic library collection within the discipline. An academic author needs to articulate an original, independent research agenda based on what is expected in the employer's RPT statement at the department or discipline level. An academic author also requires strategies for advancing a discipline, which happens through formal learning and through curated academic library collections on novel methodologies, languages, and performances in relation to author-employee expectations. An author also needs to find an academic community for general support and collegiality and also for the more formal purpose of preparing, distributing, and measuring the quality of a scholarly expression. This happens primarily through the convenings, exhibitions, and publications of scholarly societies, presses, journals, and associations.

AUTHOR-AS-CONVENER

In an academic setting, many functions contribute to the creation of a scholarly work, particularly a research journal article:

- Establishing the original research question
- Writing
- Data gathering
- Data interpreting
- Preparing an image, table, or figure

While most RPT statements will focus on individual efforts, the research endeavor has embraced group- and team-based scholarly investigation. How should an academic author, manager, publisher, or librarian navigate this type of environment? First, acknowledge that this type of authorship (i.e., team authorship) exists and can be considered as an option. Second, prepare local research policies by developing author statement templates or general authorship procedures before embarking on research or publishing and check back often as the inquiry gets underway. Third, consider the role not only of academic author but also of academic convener who brings together a unique set of people to address an important line of inquiry in a discipline or possibly across disciplines. And lastly, for individual academic authors, consider convening faculty within your department or college to discuss updating RPT require-ments to reflect the convener role that has become central to contemporary research and scholarship.

The convener role reflects the fact that one or more people can become involved in these various functions, which will necessitate group or joint au-thorship. The U.S. Copyright Office calls this type of work a "joint work" and defines it as "[. . .] a work prepared by two or more authors with the intention that their contributions be merged into inseparable or interdependent parts of a unitary whole."[19] The important term from this definition becomes *intention*. Scholarly authors need to have deliberately planned to bring their individual contributions together into a single work. Without that, there is no "joint work" and only a single-authored work with contributors. For academic units or schol-arly publishers to determine intention in order to establish authorship, they can incorporate that question into their internal policies, practices, and procedures. Academic units, department chairs, or deans can encourage group authorship through research handbooks, faculty meetings, and other research-focused events. If joint works get encouraged, the idea can be supported by establishing basic guidelines for the unit.

Authorship policies help address the level of responsibility academic authors have when sharing their ideas, or as Stephen Donovan calls it "when speaking,"[20] and define accountability to other relevant policies such as aca-demic freedom and freedom of expression as well as research integrity. Au-thorship policies also need to consider diversity, equity, and inclusion as well as copyright ownership, which we will cover in the next chapter.

NOTES

1. Roger L. Geiger. *To Advance Knowledge: The Growth of American Research Universities, 1900–1940* (New York: Oxford University Press, 1986).
2. Henry N. Drewry and Humphrey Doermann. *Stand and Prosper: Private Black Colleges and Their Students* (Princeton, NJ: Princeton University Press, 2012).
3. Miranda Jensen Haskie and Bradley Shreve. "Remembering Dine College: Origin Stories of America's First Tribal College." *Tribal College Journal of American Indian Higher Education* (August 2018), https://tribalcollegejournal.org/remembering-dine -college-origin-stories-of-americas-first-tribal-college/.
4. American Council of Learned Societies. *The First Century* (n.d.), 76, https://www .acls.org/wp-content/uploads/2021/10/The-First-Century.pdf.
5. Association for the Study of African American Life and History. "Publisher Descrip-tion" (n.d.), https://www.jstor.org/publisher/asalh, JSTOR.
6. Ty Jones. "News Release—Dine College to Re-Establish College Press." Dine College (November 18, 2018), https://www.dinecollege.edu/news-release-dine -college-to-re-establish-college-press/.

7. For a list of statements consulted, see "6-303 Supplemental Rules—Regulations Library—The University of Utah" (n.d.), https://regulations.utah.edu/academics /appendices_6/6-303_supplemental_rules.php.
8. Phil Fontanarosa, Howard Bauchner, and Annette Flanagin. "Authorship and Team Science." *JAMA* 318, no. 24 (December 26, 2017): 2433–37, https://doi.org /10.1001/jama.2017.19341.
9. The Scholarly Communications Lab provides a comprehensive study of RPT statements from a range of institutions as well as surveys to show how employment statements sometimes are at odds with the scholarly communication system. Scholarly Communications Lab | ScholCommLab. "Publications" (April 28, 2017), https://www.scholcommlab.ca/publications/.
10. Doris Bachmann-Medick. *Cultural Turns: New Orientations in the Study of Culture* (Boston: De Gruyter, 2016), 17, 103.
11. Michel Foucault. "Aesthetics, Method, and Epistemology." In *Essential Works of FOUCAULT, 1954–1984, Volume Two*, edited by James D. Faubion (New York: The New Press, 1998), 212.
12. Estelle Barrett and Barbara Bolt. *Practice as Research: Approaches to Creative Art Enquiry* (London: I. B. Tauris, 2010), 137.
13. Mark Rose. *Authors and Owners: The Invention of Copyright* (Cambridge, MA: Harvard University Press, 1993).
14. Derek J. Price. *Little Science, Big Science and Beyond . . .* (New York: Columbia University Press, 1986).
15. Eva Mroczek. *The Literary Imagination in Jewish Antiquity* (New York: Oxford University Press, 2016).
16. Damon Young. *The Art of Reading* (Melbourne: University of Melbourne Press, 2016).
17. Lisa Ede. *The Concept of Authorship: An Historical Perspective* (Philadelphia, PA: Annual Meeting of the National Council of Teachers of English, 1985), 1.
18. Ibid., 2.
19. U.S. Copyright Office. *Compendium of U.S. Copyright Office Practices, Third Edition* (Washington, DC: U.S. Copyright Office, 2021), 11.
20. Stephen Donovan, Danuta Fjellestad, and Rolf Lundén. *Authority Matters: Rethinking the Theory and Practice of Authorship* (Leiden, Netherlands: Brill, 2008), 14.

2

Elements of Copyright Ownership

Copyright ownership provides a foundation for incentivizing research, creativity, and academic authorship. Knowing its basic components provides both policy drafters and authors-as-conveners with the ability to adhere to its legalities while also ensuring equitable and inclusive approaches to the shared pursuit of investigation, inquiry, and scholarly communication. A nuanced understanding will also allow authors-as-conveners to determine the rights and responsibilities surrounding individual or independent inquiries even in a team or group setting. As a system of rights and exceptions, copyright encourages authorship, commentary, cultural and scholarly critique, and the free expression of ideas.

The robust copyright system of rights and exceptions has developed over time since the first Copyright Act in 1790. While there was a federal law, neither the Library of Congress nor the U.S. Copyright Office existed in 1790, both of which provide the registration system today. Instead of a centralized office, authors had to register their works with the clerks of district courts. Protections extended to limited categories of works (maps, charts, and books) and terms lasted only fourteen years with one renewal term of fourteen years. Today the term is life of the author plus seventy years.

One of the first copyright entries in 1790 came from an academic author, a teacher named John Barry who lived in Pennsylvania.[1] The registered work was called *The Philadelphia Spelling Book*. One of the first joint copyright registrations came from co-authors Absalom Jones and Richard Allen, both of whom lived in Pennsylvania and had formerly been enslaved. The registered work was titled *A Narrative of the Proceedings of the Black People, During the Late Awful Calamity in Philadelphia, in the Year 1793*.[2] Other significant firsts included Elise Hamilton, first female songwriter to register a copyright in 1870 for a waltz named *Isola Bella*, and Sarah Winnemucca (Northern Paiute), first American Indian copyright holder in 1883 for her book *Life Among the Piutes: Their Wrongs and Claims*.[3, 4] Undoubtedly many other firsts from BIPOC authors have occurred, but uncovering them all becomes its own research specialization given copyright law's decentralized history. (The Library of Congress has digitized many of the historic copyright registration records, including registrations made under state laws. Those scans have been made in collaboration with law librarian Zvi Rosen.[5])

For purposes of this chapter, we will focus on several elements of copyright ownership that become relevant for academic authors and related policies, the most salient being the basic definition of copyright protection, shared authorship, and works-for-hire. To fully answer the question of when an academic author becomes a copyright holder, we will need to look to the current U.S. Copyright Act as well as components within institutional policies.

The elements of copyright ownership within today's Copyright Act applicable to academic authors include:

- Copyrightability
- Exclusive rights
- Work-for-hire
- Joint authorship
- Compilations and collected works

Elements of copyright ownership related to academic authorship that stems from institutional policies include:

- Types of copyrightable work
- Students' rights as authors
- Academic freedom

THE U.S. COPYRIGHT ACT

COPYRIGHTABILITY

The Copyright Act provides the terms for copyright ownership within the United States, defining aspects such as work-for-hire and shared authorship, while institutional policies denote interpretations of the Copyright Act, specifically as they relate to employees and the works they create.

To start with, the basic definition of copyright comes directly from the first section of the Copyright Act:[6]

> Copyright protection subsists, in accordance with this title, in original works of authorship fixed in any tangible medium of expression, now known or later developed, from which they can be perceived, reproduced, or otherwise communicated, either directly or with the aid of a machine or device. Works of authorship include the following categories:
>
> 1. literary works;
> 2. musical works, including any accompanying words;
> 3. dramatic works, including any accompanying music;

4. pantomimes and choreographic works;
5. pictorial, graphic, and sculptural works;
6. motion pictures and other audiovisual works;
7. sound recordings; and
8. architectural works.

In no case does copyright protection for an original work of authorship extend to any idea, procedure, process, system, method of operation, concept, principle, or discovery, regardless of the form in which it is described, explained, illustrated, or embodied in such work.

Essentially, most original text-based and any audiovisual works become eligible for copyright protection. Ideas, principles, and discoveries do not. Since academic authors work within ideas and discoveries, this becomes an important distinction within institutional copyright ownership policies that get created. Conveying that the expression of an idea or discovery gets protected will become useful for academic authors.

Including examples of works within these broad categories could also be helpful. For example, table 2.1 shows what the U.S. Copyright Office *Compendium of U.S. Copyright Office Practices* lists as types of literary and audiovisual works and the various media in which authors can fix expressions:[7]

Table 2.1. Types of Literary and Audiovisual Work

Literary Works	Audiovisual Works	Possible Media to Embody Expressions
Fiction	Lectures	Paper
Nonfiction	Interviews	Canvas
Poetry	Musical works	Clay
Directories	Sound recordings	Stone
Catalogs	Dramatic works	Metal
Textbooks	Choreographic works	Film
Reference works	Videogames	Digital files
Compilations of information	Motion pictures	Constructed buildings
Computer programs	Painting	
Databases	Sculpture	
Advertising copy	Graphic art	
	Photographs	
	Prints	
	Art reproductions	
	Maps and globes	
	Charts and diagrams	
	Technical drawings	

A scholarly author or research group could potentially create several copyrightable works within one project area: nonfiction works such as books, journal articles, posters, a database, an online exhibit, a website, even a podcast or other online performance. Noting authorship and keeping track of copyright ownership on multiple types of works has become a crucial aspect of contemporary scholarship as academic authors more commonly perform their roles as conveners.

EXCLUSIVE RIGHTS

Through the U.S. Copyright Act, authors receive the following rights in their original works of authorship:

1. to reproduce the copyrighted work in copies or phonorecords;
2. to prepare derivative works based upon the copyrighted work;
3. to distribute copies or phonorecords of the copyrighted work to the public by sale or other transfer of ownership, or by rental, lease, or lending;
4. in the case of literary, musical, dramatic, and choreographic works, pantomimes, and motion pictures and other audiovisual works, to perform the copyrighted work publicly;
5. in the case of literary, musical, dramatic, and choreographic works, pantomimes, and pictorial, graphic, or sculptural works, including the individual images of a motion picture or other audiovisual work, to display the copyrighted work publicly; and
6. in the case of sound recordings, to perform the copyrighted work publicly by means of a digital audio transmission.[8]

In the role of author-as-convener, academic authors will need to be aware generally of these rights (as well as copyrightability) as they work with other authors outside of their institution and as they work with different categories of authors within their own institution. As employees, these ownership rights will become germane within the institution's copyright ownership policies. Copyright ownership policies define the work-for-hire element found within the Copyright Act.

WORK-FOR-HIRE

The Copyright Act defines a work-for-hire as "a work prepared by an employee within the scope of his or her employment." The two relevant sections—initial ownership and works made for hire—get spelled out further in chapter 2 of the Copyright Act:

Initial Ownership—Copyright in a work protected under this title vests initially in the author or authors of the work. The authors of a joint work are co-owners [sic] of copyright in the work.

Works Made for Hire—In the case of a work made for hire, the employer or other person for whom the work was prepared is considered the author for purposes of this title, and, unless the parties have expressly agreed otherwise in a written instrument signed by them, owns all of the rights comprised in the copyright.[9]

As we saw in chapter 1, academic authors get impacted by all of the elements present in these definitions: originality, embodying an expression in tangible medium, and author-as-employee.

JOINT AUTHORSHIP, COMPILATIONS, AND COLLECTED WORKS

Each of these elements get treated separately within the Copyright Act, but they are all closely related when it comes to development of authorship policies. As we saw in chapter 1, joint authorship gets defined as "[. . .] a work prepared by two or more authors with the intention that their contributions be merged into inseparable or interdependent parts of a unitary whole."[10] The "inseparable" and "interdependent" pieces of the definition of a joint work are what distinguish those types of works from compilations and collected works. Many academic authors will engage in preparing compilations and collected works so understanding this distinction and conveying the details via authorship policies will be important.

Intention will also become an underlying factor of both copyright ownership and authorship. As the Copyright Act spells out, the authors of a jointly authored work will need to determine beforehand how their independent contributions will merge into a singular, cohesive original work of authorship. For authors-as-employees and authors-as-conveners, these conversations will need to occur early in the scholarly communication process and, ideally, be informed by policies as well as these general principles of copyright ownership. That process, essentially, is what an authorship policy becomes: a statement of principles held by the author-as-employee and author-as-convener.

As we have seen, jointly authored works have a specific definition. They are types of works distinct from compilations. Compilations, which many academic authors create, get defined this way in the Copyright Act:[11]

A "compilation" is a work formed by the collection and assembling of pre-existing materials or of data that are selected, coordinated, or arranged in such a way that the resulting work as a whole constitutes an original work of authorship. The term "compilation" includes collective works.

The *Compendium* indicates that compilations usually contain the following distinct forms of authorship:

- Selection
- Coordination
- Arrangement

Selection authorship relates to "choosing the material or data that will be included in the compilations." Coordination authorship includes the "classifying, categorizing, ordering, or grouping [of] the material or data. Arrangement authorship [involves the] organizing or moving [of the] order, position, or placement of [the] material or data within the compilation as a whole."[12]

These types of authorships (selection, coordination, arrangement) can potentially happen on a regular basis across many academic institutions. A solo academic author could engage in this authorship, but more likely an author-as-convener will help oversee other academic authors working on these various compilations. Compilation authorship versus joint authorship will, again, depend on the agreements (i.e. authorship policy or plan) beforehand and also depend on the final output and product. The *Compendium* clarifies further that the compilation itself needs to "qualify" as a literary or audiovisual work with a focus on "the manner in which the material or data have been selected, coordinated, and arranged . . . with sufficient originality to warrant protection."[13]

A research group spanning institutions in order to compile pre-existing data for purposes of a new analysis or arrangement would want to consider compilation as a type of work of authorship. The authorship policy would help spell out the preference of compilation over joint authorship and delve deeper into distinct authorship assignments. For example, asking who will perform the selection authorship, who will embark on the coordination authorship, and who will enact the arrangement authorship. The same process could be followed for determining the joint authorship of the journal article, poster, or book, but instead the intention will be to bring together all the writing assignments into a singular work with multiple authors. The research group would then, potentially, have a copyrightable work in the compilation of data and a copyrightable work in the journal article and poster.

INSTITUTIONAL POLICIES

TYPES OF COPYRIGHTABLE WORKS

Authors-as-employees will want to determine which type of copyrightable works get covered by their institution's copyright ownership policy and also determine how employee categorizations affect the ownership of works-for-hire. Look for the categories listed above that come from the U.S. Copyright Act. Next, authors will want to look for any specific listing of types of copyrightable works within those categories, such as books, journal articles, software, databases, presentations, lectures, and syllabi. They are sometimes referred to as "traditional scholarly works." These types of copyrightable works will most likely receive special treatment based on employee type. Employees categorized as faculty will have slightly different ownership rules than employees categorized as staff or student-employees.

STUDENTS' RIGHTS AS AUTHORS

An academic author-as-convener will want to make the distinction in any authorship policy regarding student-authored works. The institution's copyright ownership policy will detail what students—who are not employees—own, which should be all of the exclusive rights. Students, as non-employees, are not subject to the usual work-for-hire distinction within the U.S. Copyright Act. Instead, the basic principles of copyright protection remain relevant for students, as does their own academic freedom as established by the institution's policies.

Many academic institutions have student codes or student bill of rights, which an author-as-convener will want to consult when developing an authorship policy. The 1967 *Joint Statement on Rights and Freedoms of Students* developed by the American Association of University Professors (AAUP), the United States Student Association (USSA), and others provided the underlying principles to help inform these policies.[14] The statement approaches free expression from the perspective of pursuing knowledge as well as its creation and transmission. Creating and transmitting knowledge is where copyright ownership and freedom of expression intersect and overlap.

For research administrators developing a copyright ownership policy, becoming familiar with the general principles of copyright ownership as well as its connection to freedom of expression and academic freedom will be paramount. Freedom of expression in higher education (grounded in the First Amendment to the U.S. Constitution) usually gets defined as examining and communicating ideas by lawful means. R. Chace Ramey in *Student First Amendment Speech and Expression Rights: Armbands to Bong HiTS* provides more specification and indicates that freedom of expression for students

> encompasses student speech; student press; student verbal and non-verbal expressive actions; distribution of petitions, literature, and flyers; cyber communication including internet blogs, social networking profiles, email, instant messenger, and texting; participation in saluting the flag; and expression through student attire.[15]

Publishing—a technical term which gets defined as providing multiple copies of a work to the public for sale or for free—exists as a means of realizing one's freedom of speech and expression. Even works not provided to the public that remain unpublished still act as a form of exercising free speech and expression. Moreover, the U.S. Copyright Act does not limit copyright protection by age of the author. Essentially, the general definition of copyright protection detailed above would apply to learners, and mirroring these rights within a copyright ownership policy becomes necessary in a higher education and research setting.

For students who have employment within a research group or area, the work-for-hire aspect will become applicable. The academic author managing the research program can consult the copyright ownership policy to determine the ownership rules regarding faculty-staff joint works. Those details will, in turn, inform the research group's approaches to authorship, ideally in the form of a written authorship policy.

ACADEMIC FREEDOM

Freedom to pursue truth and knowledge is where freedom of expression and academic freedom tend to meet. Pursuing knowledge encompasses learning (both inside and outside a classroom), but it can also involve independent research and investigation. Having the leeway to investigate becomes endemic to the full spectrum of academic freedom because, as we saw in chapter 1, the motivating structure of the institution pushes scholars to communicate findings from research pursuits. And the premise behind the institutional motivating factor to encourage research and communication stems from the initial idea behind copyright in the United States "to promote the progress of science and useful arts, by securing for limited times to authors and inventors the exclusive right to their respective writings and discoveries."[16]

While this did not establish a *right* to engage in scientific and artistic pursuits, it certainly incentivized it by offering legal rights to the output of the pursuits. (James Herrick argues that the free exercise of religion clause of the First Amendment also included the freedom of religious inquiry, which could be a foundation of any idea of a right to scientific inquiry.[17]) As universities and colleges in the United States evolved, any type of right to inquire built up with that growth through community norms, standards, and eventually policies and procedures regarding employment expectations to conduct research as detailed in the first chapter. Codifying students' rights to independently inquire and pursue truth soon followed with the formation of the United States National Student Association in 1947 and the AAUP/USSA joint statement referenced above.

As such, a special exemption for traditional scholarly works as a type of work-for-hire has existed since the early 1900s as the principles of academic freedom began to emerge within the United States.[18] As the teaching profession evolved into a teaching and research profession (see chapter 1), the necessity of ensuring that professors had the ability to communicate and publish their findings to fellow professors became essential.

As we saw in the definition of work-for-hire above, the institution itself would own the copyright in the works produced by employees. But to have someone at the institution besides the author determine publication readiness could potentially constrain professors' freedom to seek a scholarly critique and the eventual dissemination of their works of authorship.

In the next chapter, we will explore the connection between copyright and research further by introducing the broader domain of scholarly communication and how authorship operates within that system.

NOTES

1. Daniel Gilbert. "Pennsylvania: The Birthplace of Copyright Law." Pennsylvania Center for the Book (Fall 2010), https://pabook.libraries.psu.edu/literary-cultural-heri tage-map-pa/feature-articles/pennsylvania-birthplace-copyright-law.
2. Molly O'Hagan Hardy. "Figures of Authorship in Mathew Carey's Transatlantic Yellow Fever Pamphlets." *Book History* 17, no. 1 (2014): 221–49, https://doi.org /10.1353/bh.2014.0003.
3. Alison Hall. "Celebrating Women's History Month: Female Songwriters." *Copyright Notices* (March 2018), https://www.copyright.gov/history/lore/pdfs/201803%20 CLore_March2018.pdf.
4. Wendy A. Maloney. "Bridge-Building Native American Registers Early Copyright." *Copyright Notices* (April 2009), https://www.copyright.gov/history/lore/pdfs /200904%20CLore_April2009.pdf?loclr=eanco.
5. Library of Congress. "Early Copyright Records Collection, 1790 to 1870."
6. U.S. Copyright Office. "Copyright Law of the United States," https://www.copyright .gov/title17/92chap1.html#101.
7. U.S. Copyright Office. *Compendium of U.S. Copyright Office Practices, Third Edition.* Washington, DC: U.S. Copyright Office, 2021, 4.
8. U.S. Copyright Office. "Copyright Law of the United States." https://www.copyright .gov/title17/92chap1.html#101.
9. U.S. Copyright Office. "Copyright Law of the United States." https://www.copyright .gov/title17/92chap2.html.
10. U.S. Copyright Office. *Compendium of U.S. Copyright Office Practices, Third Edition* (Washington, DC: U.S. Copyright Office, 2021), 11.
11. U.S. Copyright Office. "Copyright Law of the United States." https://www.copyright .gov/title17/92chap1.html#101.
12. U.S. Copyright Office. *Compendium of U.S. Copyright Office Practices, Third Edition* (Washington, DC: U.S. Copyright Office, 2021), 18.
13. Ibid.
14. American Association of University Professors and United States Student Association. *Joint Statement on Rights and Freedoms of Students* (November 1992), https:// www.aaup.org/report/joint-statement-rights-and-freedoms-students.

15. R. Chace Ramey. *Student First Amendment Speech and Expression Rights: Armbands to Bong HiTS* (El Paso, TX: LFB Scholarly Publishing, 2011), 1.
16. Frank Evina. "Copyright Lore." *Copyright Notices* (September 2004), https://www.copyright.gov/history/lore/pdfs/200409%20CLore_September2004.pdf.
17. James A. Herrick. "The English Deists' Argument for Freedom of Expression: Religious Inquiry and the First Amendment." *Free Speech Yearbook* 34 (1996): 131–40.
18. Hans-Jeorg Tiede. *University Reform* (Baltimore, MD: Johns Hopkins University Press, 2015).

3

Authorship, Copyright, Scholarly Communication

This chapter focuses on the connections between authorship, copyright, and scholarly communication. Since the first two chapters provided details on authorship and copyright, we will look more in-depth at scholarly communication in this chapter, but with attention on how the three become connected.

Scholarly communication, as a term, has come to define the system used to convey information resulting from deliberate and sustained inquiry and investigation. It becomes a specific type of information concentrated on the nature of the original data or primary source.

Within other types of information such as mass communication or journalism, for example, the emphasis becomes the facts involved in an event. Professional or trade communication, as another type of communication, delivers various approaches to engaging in a profession, including assessing its outcomes or developing new processes or procedures. With scholarly communication, the information highlights original data and the circumstances and context around the finding of the data or primary source, either its historical origin or some type of original observation in nature or in a setting involving people. Unlike other forms of communication, scholarly communication also shows how the primary source or original data relate to other findings, both present and past.

The system supports the communication of inquiry-based information to an audience of those who use similar investigation techniques, making the publication scope somewhat narrow. (The audience can also include learners and general information seekers, but they become a secondary audience.) It consists of two primary communication means, verbal and written, but with multiple venue and distribution options such as small gatherings or large convenings, conferences as well as journals, books, reports/websites/databases, oral histories, and art, all of which get detailed below. Many of the communicators and audiences active within the scholarly communication system serve as employees in universities and colleges. They can also be employed by stand-alone research entities such as institutes, centers, and think tanks or act as independent, solo researchers or as members of Tribal and First Nations.

While the communicators within the scholarly communication system might be limited in the scope of their publication audiences, they still act as authors. As we saw in the last chapter, certain legalities through the federal Copyright Act further define authorship as well as ownership of works. While authorship, broadly speaking, encompasses all types of communications, not just scholarly, the ownership aspects of authorship become relevant to the scholarly communication system. Where they primarily intersect resides in legalities and policies. The policies of the publication and distribution venues become just as important as the policies of the institutions that employ scholarly authors. Those policies become informed by the Copyright Act, essentially providing the foundation to enable the scholarly communication system. Together, the Copyright Act and the scholarly communication system, with its various publication venues, limited audiences, and sites of employment, coalesce to form a tailored definition of authorship, which we saw in the first chapter.

As we also saw in chapter 1, academic authorship is changing. Scholarly authors act as conveners just as often (or perhaps even more often) than they act as solo authors. Those that the scholarly author brings together will have

Scholarly Authors	Publishers
• Authors-as-Employees • Authors-as-Conveners • Student authors • Independent authors	• Societies • Presses • Corporate • Institutions
Librarians + Libraries	Archivists + Archives
Scholarly Art Exhibitors	Scholarly Performance Organizers

Figure 3.1. People within the Scholarly Communication System

their own authorship roles—be it research designer, image creator, writer, compiler, storyteller—and together they will own the work of authorship. Depending on policies of the institution, the author-as-convener might get to decide if and when the work of authorship gets communicated or published, but that does not also mean that the author-as-convener is the sole owner of the copyrightable work. Authorship policies help bring together both the Copyright Act and institutional policies in order to acknowledge these important distinctions.

THE SCHOLARLY COMMUNICATION SYSTEM

To support scholarly authors' exchange of research results, various communication and publishing possibilities exist through societies, publishers, and presses as well as libraries and librarians who, together with archives and archivists and their institutions, serve as the underlying foundation of the system. Let's look at how authorship and copyright ownership work within the various communication and publishing options offered by societies, publishers, libraries, and archives, such as conferences, journals, books, reports, databases, websites, art, and oral histories.

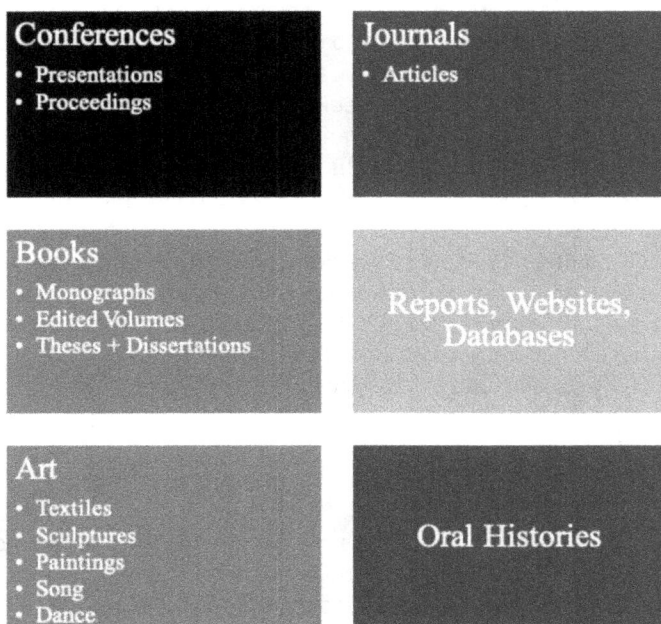

Figure 3.2. Works within the Scholarly Communication System

CONFERENCES

Societies and associations organize conferences in order to provide a forum for academic authors to present findings. The gatherings establish a community-based network of people who study similar topics using similar research methods. The society (or other independent entity that may organize a conference) becomes the publisher and the presenter creating and submitting a proposal becomes the author. As we saw in chapter 1, many different types of learned societies operate today. As a publisher, societies and conference organizers obtain copyright permissions from authors usually at the time of submission or registration. If a society or conference does not have this in place, they can consider developing these terms in collaboration with a copyright attorney.

In terms of copyright ownership, two activities within conferences become relevant: creating a presentation and presenting. Through the process of fixing an expression of an idea into a tangible medium, a presentation becomes a work of authorship protected through the U.S. Copyright Act. The right to publicly perform and publicly display the work would be with the author. The right to reproduce the work in copies, which could also become relevant for a conference (especially an online conference or one with an associated publication), would also be with the author. Authors-as-employees will want to consult their institution's copyright ownership policies about presentations so they have a full understanding of what they can agree to in the process of submitting a proposal or the presentation itself. Most conferences need only permission—as opposed to an assignment of rights—to display and perform the presentation.

Authorship policies can be rare for a conference, but for societies with an associated publication, such as proceedings or special journal issues, they can become relevant. In those instances, an authorship policy would ask authors to indicate whether or not the work is a joint work of authorship (i.e., that everyone has participated in creating the work) and which of the authors will present the material. A society contemplating a conference publication to accompany a conference should consider developing an authorship policy to provide this type of important guidance to the presenters who will participate. For conferences without a publication, the focus usually remains on conference or publication policies that ask attendees to agree to copyright-related terms, such as not fully copying others' works without permission and not distributing full works without permission.

JOURNALS

While conferences seek to bring academic authors together for a time-limited event to share scholarly communications, journals provide a more frequent mechanism. Journal issues get published multiple times a year, usually publish several papers within each issue, and get distributed throughout the world. A society (or other publishing entity such as a corporate publisher) will oversee the journal's production by appointed editors and peer reviewers and, as with conferences, will act as the publisher.

Like conferences, publishers of journals will obtain copyright permission from authors, but instead of permission to perform or display the work, the right to copy and distribute the work will be sought. A tradition of seeking an assignment of rights instead of simply permissions has built up over time within journal publishing. Some journals will seek exclusive permission in order to become the sole publisher and others will operate under an open access or shared ownership principle where the rights stay with the author(s); the journal will ask that everyone get permission to reuse, including the publisher, and that both the authors and the journal get attributed as the rights holders and the publisher, respectively. For journals looking to implement or change their publishing policies, this book provides some of that initial guidance, but legal advice should be obtained.

As we saw in chapter 2, papers exist as works of authorship protected through the U.S. Copyright Act. Papers are also usually considered traditional scholarly works within institutional copyright ownership policies. This is based on the history of scholarly communication we saw in chapter 1. Academic authors should still consult copyright ownership policies for guidance and, even more valuable, consult any institutional or local research-group authorship policies.

Authorship policies are very common for journals. Such policies help establish clarity on roles and responsibilities within the scholarly communication system. The journal system has seen a significant increase in the number of authors on a paper, and in response to what has come to be called "gifting of authorship," journals have put authorship policies in place.[1] They ask that only those who can discuss or defend the research be listed as an author. Authorship policies, unlike publication agreements, are not legal contracts per se but, instead, are operational, educational, and guidance documents that provide information and direction to authors seeking to communicate their findings through a journal.

BOOKS

With books, as with journals, academic authors seek to communicate ideas by entering into agreements with publishers to make copies of an underlying work of authorship accessible throughout the world. Books, including theses and dissertations, get issued less frequently than journals and typically reflect an individual author's findings on a single topic (i.e., a monograph). Books within the scholarly communication system can also include edited volumes which show several authors' stand-alone findings within a subject area brought together by an editor. The editor of such a volume would follow a type of publication agreement usually labeled a contributor agreement (book publishers seeking to establish contributor agreements for edited volumes should obtain legal advice from a copyright attorney). The work becomes a single copyrighted work with one title, one editor, one publisher, but with various authors all of whom get listed as individual authors within the volume.

Books, including theses and dissertations, receive copyright protection through the U.S. Copyright Act. Like papers, they are considered traditional scholarly works within institutional copyright ownership policies applicable to authors-as-employees. For theses and dissertations written by student authors who are not employees, the institution typically does not have a work-for-hire basis for claiming copyright ownership, as we saw in chapter 2.

For book manuscripts resulting from multiple contributors from the same institutional research group or from student contributions, the author-as-employee will want to consider the institution's extant authorship policies as well as copyright ownership policies. If none exist, the author-as-employee could develop a local policy that will help guide the determination of co-authorship of the book manuscript or to consider working with the publisher on utilizing formal contributor agreements.

Developing a local authorship policy could become more central because authorship policies at the level of the book publisher are less common. This is simply because there tend to be fewer authors associated with a book. And when there are multiple authors, a legal agreement (instead of a policy) gets utilized to convey authorship.

REPORTS, WEBSITES, DATABASES

Reports, websites, and databases represent additional ways for academic authors to convey their findings. While conferences, journals, and books will typically have a publisher outside the author's institution, these types of works often get published by the institution where the author is affiliated. The entity where the author works will become the publisher by providing the web servers and other internet architecture needed to distribute digital or digitized works. When that is the case, the institution will need to employ a copyright ownership policy, an authorship policy, and potentially a copying of copyrighted works policy (see *Copyright Policies & Workflows in Libraries: A Concise Handbook* for details on copyright reuse policies).

Reports, websites, and databases all represent copyrightable works of authorship that receive protection through the U.S. Copyright Act. They do not, however, always represent traditional scholarly works vis-à-vis institutional copyright ownership policies. Authors-as-employees will want to closely read the institution's copyright ownership policy. And for administrators overseeing copyright ownership policies, including these types of scholarly works in the policy will be beneficial for the sake of clarity. Academic authors developing reports, websites, or databases alongside students or other faculty should consult both the institutional copyright ownership policy as well as a local authorship policy for guidance on how to arrive at a contribution of authorship.

ART

While fewer scholars will use art as a scholarly communication device as compared to books, conference presentations, and journal articles, it nonetheless represents a significant and powerful way for researchers to communicate findings. From textiles to paintings to sculptures to song and dance, art can be a mechanism to convey the results of sustained inquiry and observation.

Textiles, paintings, sculptures, song, movement all represent copyrightable works of authorship protected through the U.S. Copyright Act. Like conference presentations, copyright in art can also involve public performance and public display through the process of exhibition and showcase. Depending on the institution, some copyright ownership policies might consider art as a traditional scholarly work, but some may not. Academic authors will want to consult their institution's policy regarding copyright ownership of art. Administrators overseeing copyright ownership or authorship policies will want to consider including works of art as a traditional scholarly work.

Many exhibitors of scholarly art exist, but compared to other types of works of authorship, there are fewer scholarly art publishers. To publish art means to provide more than one copy of an original work for free or for sale to the general public.[2] Often, scholarly art does not get reproduced in copies. Instead, it gets publicly displayed or publicly performed. Scholarly art galleries will exhibit a textile, sculpture, or painting. Or a scholarly venue will prepare an event for a song or dance performance. Permission would be needed from the academic author to display or perform the work, but a performance does not mean a work has been published. This makes authorship policies essential for a performance venue.

Authorship policies for scholarly art exhibitors might not be as common, but they will be crucial. This is because, as a type of author, visual artists also have an additional right to claim authorship (i.e., the right to be associated with a work) and the right to not be associated with a work (i.e., to not be considered the author of a work) "in the event of a distortion, mutilation, or other modification of the work which would be prejudicial to his or her [or their] honor or reputation [. . .]."[3] A scholarly art exhibitor will want to consider this aspect of the U.S. Copyright Act and work closely with a copyright attorney on crafting a legal agreement for exhibition and authorship.

ORAL HISTORIES

Establishing events to facilitate the sharing of oral histories represents a common cultural practice among Indigenous communities as well as a research method for Indigenous scholars.[4] Often these oral histories do not get fixed in a tangible medium so copyright protection might not get enacted, but they represent an important research method as well as a moment of authorship. The event itself becomes both the methodology as well as the scholarly communication output. The entity organizing or holding the performance event would essentially become the "publisher," and while copies of works might not be distributed, having a policy to acknowledge source or authorship would be important. Much like a conference schedule, a program announcing an oral history event that might get developed could become a copyrightable work of authorship. Such a document could be used to convey the names of the participating authors and the names or nature of their oral histories.

If the oral histories do get fixed in a tangible medium, an authorship policy would help clarify ownership. As we saw in chapter 2, the person who makes the recording becomes the copyright holder, and in an oral history event, the storyteller may not have envisioned this potential ownership situation by simply agreeing to participate in the event. The event organizers would want to be transparent about the event details and obtain permission from a privacy perspective and also have permission-sharing options when it comes to recording. If permission is received to record and the next goal is to make copies of and distribute the recordings, that would become its own publication agreement. An oral history event organizer or scholar would want to obtain legal advice from a copyright attorney or tribal committee in order to establish a publication agreement.

CULTURE OF THE SCHOLARLY COMMUNICATION SYSTEM

COMPETITION AND SYSTEMIC INEQUITIES

As we saw in chapter 1, academic authors have often been associated with institutions of higher learning as employees. Authors-as-employees work closely with colleagues and students at the institution as well as those across the discipline. As part of the RPT employment process, academic authors-as-employees also must prove themselves to those same groups as well as to administrators. The employment expectations in and of themselves can create ambitious environments, although promotion and tenure judgments with regard to employment performance are envisioned as being germane to only the individual (and not in comparison to others), but nonetheless, a competitive spirit has emerged as part of the scholarly communication system through the academic tenure process. Part of the culture gets informed by the desire of academic institutions to compete with one another as well: competition for students, employees, and for overall reputation or strength in a certain area. The culture of the institution can drive the actions of its employees and, in turn, influence the culture of a much larger system of fellow scholarly communicators and audiences.

The institutions of higher learning where academic authors have employ-ment have also historically been predominantly White colleges and universi-ties, as we saw in chapter 1. According to Ozlem Sensoy and Robin DiAngelo, the breakdown of faculty conducting research within the United States as professors in 2013 was as follows:

> 84 percent of full-time professors were White (58 percent males and 26 percent females), 4 percent Black, 3 percent Hispanic, and 9 percent Asian/ Pacific Islander. Making up less than 1 percent each were professors who were American Indian/Alaska Native and of two or more races.[5]

In 2020, the National Center for Education Statistics indicated that 79 percent of faculty conducting research were White (51 percent males and 28 percent females), 4 percent Black, 4 percent Hispanic, 12 percent Asian/Pacific Islander, and less than 1 percent American Indian/Alaska Native and two or more races.[6]

Authors active within the scholarly communication system will essentially reflect the employment within institutions of higher learning, as will librarians and archivists. The American Library Association and Society of American Archivists indicate the following demographics in 2010 and 2015: 88 percent of full-time librarians and archivists were White (83 percent females and 17 percent males), 5 percent Black, 3 percent Hispanic, 3 percent Asian/Pacific Islander, and less than 1 percent American Indian/Alaska Native and two or more races.[7, 8]

Similar statistics can be seen within the scholarly publishing component of the scholarly communication system. In Paul Hirsch's 1992 study of owner-ship of media companies, he found that many U.S. publishing companies be-came "new divisions of British or German parent [companies]" in the 1980s.[9] Albert Greco, Robert Wharton, and Amy Brand found in 2016 that 91 percent of scholarly publishing professionals across thirty-three nations "identified themselves as white."[10]

Based on these statistics, one could argue that the scholarly communica-tion system has operated as a historically and predominantly White system lacking in racial and ethnic diversity. Racism and sexism within the system have also occurred, such as helicopter research where minoritized and marginalized populations get studied by members from the majority population without full input or involvement.[11] Research by female scholars often gets dismissed, un-acknowledged, or plagiarized.[12] Students' authorship contributions have been co-opted by principal investigators or supervising faculty.[13]

A potential way administrators, publishers, librarians, and authors-as-conveners can address these past (and ongoing) inequities is to write clear policies with equity in mind. While it is naïve to think that a policy can right a wrong such as White supremacy, racism, or sexism, a policy can help prevent a systemically inequitable issue get acknowledged with the goal of providing a new direction.

In the next chapter, we will detail how to develop good policies that establish a more fair scholarly communication system and to ensure more just acknowledgment of authorship and authorship contribution within the research endeavor.

NOTES

1. William B. Weeks, Amy E. Wallace, and B. C. Surott Kimberly. "Changes in Authorship Patterns in Prestigious US Medical Journals." *Social Science & Medicine* 59, no. 9 (November 1, 2004): 1949-54, https://doi.org/10.1016/j.socscimed.2004.02.029.
2. William S. Strong. *The Copyright Book*, 6th ed. (Cambridge, MA: MIT Press, 2014).
3. U.S. Copyright Office. "Copyright Law of the United States." https://www.copyright.gov/title17/92chap1.html.
4. Sweeney Windchief and Timothy San Pedro, eds. *Applying Indigenous Research Methods: Storying with Peoples and Communities* (Milton, UK: Taylor & Francis, 2019).
5. Ozlem Sensoy and Robin DiAngelo. "'We Are All for Diversity, but . . .': How Faculty Hiring Committees Reproduce Whiteness and Practical Suggestions for How They Can Change." *Harvard Educational Review* 87, no. 4 (Winter 2017): 557-80.
6. National Center for Education Statistics. "Condition of Education—Characteristics of Postsecondary Faculty" (2020), https://nces.ed.gov/programs/coe/indicator/csc/postsecondary-faculty.
7. American Library Association. *Librarianship & Library Staff Statistics* (2010), https://www.ala.org/aboutala/sites/ala.org.aboutala/files/content/diversity/diversitycounts/diversitycountstables2012.pdf.
8. Society of American Archivists. *2015 SAA Employment Survey* (2015), http://files.archivists.org/membership/surveys/employment2015/SAA-EmploymentSurvey2015-summary_0615.pdf.
9. Paul M. Hirsch. "Globalization of Mass Media Ownership." *Communication Research* 19, no. 6 (1992): 677-81.
10. Albert N. Greco, R.M. Wharton, and Amy Brand. "Demographics of Scholarly Publishing and Communication Professionals." *Learned Publishing*, 29 (2016): 97-101, https://doi.org/10.1002/leap.1017.
11. Linda Tuhiwai Smith. *Decolonizing Methodologies, Third ed.* (London: Bloomsbury Academic & Professional, 2021).
12. Kirsti Cole and Holly Hassel. *Surviving Sexism in Academia* (Milton, UK: Taylor & Francis, 2017).
13. Delma M. Ramos and Yi Varaxy. "Doctoral Women of Color Coping with Racism and Sexism in the Academy." *International Journal of Doctoral Studies* 15 (2020): 135-58, https://doi.org/10.28945/4508.

4

Best Practices in Developing Policies

In this chapter, we will look at best practices for developing a policy as an author-as-employee for a research group, as a research administrator at an institution, or as someone working within a publishing entity or scholarly communication venue. Generally, policies provide guidance on the actions a group of people can undertake within a workplace setting or professional gathering. They provide a common definition of terms, a description of general expectations, and details of any prohibitions, allowances, or exceptions to either. The main feature becomes the scope or purpose of the policy.

CREATE A CLEAR POLICY PURPOSE

Defining a policy's purpose establishes the foundation to help bring all of the components together. Give yourself a sufficient amount of time to develop the policy's purpose. Depending on the number of people the policy will impact, you may need several months of conversation to fully develop the purpose. Policies impacting smaller groups of people may take less time.

Start with a simple statement: "This policy assists X research group with determining authorship on papers, presentations, book chapters, websites, databases and other scholarly works produced by the group" or "This policy applies to contributors at X scholarly conference." The beginning statement will be more complex for institution-wide or company-wide policies: "This policy directs those at X institution on ownership of works of authorship" or "This policy conveys authorship requirements for X publisher."

Establishing the policy statement can be the most challenging step in the entire process. It will be iterative. It will feel frustrating at times with the slow pace and with moments of confusion and uncertainty, but there is nothing wrong with that type of activity. Resist the temptation to abandon the process. Seek out advice and consult good policy-writing books and other resources mentioned throughout this chapter.

Authors-as-conveners could ask fellow research managers for their authorship (or related) policies and talk through them together, especially about ways the policy may have helped (or hurt) a real-life situation. Consider utilizing academic or discipline-based social media sites to ask if other research managers have worked on developing similar policies and look for research manager networks or mentoring programs within your research university or institute. The Society of Research Administrators International brings together research managers from across the world to share resources and information about the role of managing a research project. This book offers sample policies as well, but combining those with information from those in similar situations or those within your institution will result in more detailed, relevant, and applicable insight.

Research administrators crafting a policy purpose can also work closely with other similarly situated professionals. Research universities will have research administration offices and locating professional associations such as the National Council of University Research Administrators will provide a network of peers. Publishers and scholarly communication venues will want to engage in professional conferences to get insight from peers. Groups such as the Society for Scholarly Publishing, Council of Scientific Editors, American Council of Learned Societies, Association of University Presses, Committee on Publication Ethics, and Open Access Scholarly Publishing Association all represent excellent resources.

With a draft purpose statement in hand, the next step would include asking closely or similarly situated peers about their experiences regarding the policy topic. For example, for a lab or research group authorship policy, an author-as-convener would want to ask other research managers about any authorship issues they may have experienced in the past to help get a more fully informed perspective. Research administrators would consult with their peers at other institutions. Publishers, editors, or scholarly communication venue hosts would consult widely with a range of peers: fellow editors, other publishing professionals, and even studio or art gallery professionals who have experience in working with authors, artists, and other copyright holders. Table 4.1 lists resources for finding similarly situated peers.

Conversations with others will continue to influence the purpose statement. Perhaps the policy purpose will include more than one element, for example. Using the example statement above, it is possible for a policy to determine authorship and to also set rules about who will decide when publishing the results of the research group will occur. Such a statement could say: "This policy assists X research group with determining authorship on papers, presentations, book chapters, websites, databases, and other scholarly works produced by the group. It also determines the role of the convener or research manager in determining readiness of publication." Allow development of the purpose statement the necessary amount of time to reflect the overall goal of the research group or institution and rewrite the purpose statement as needed. Build in time for this process as it will continue to change as you have additional conversations with others.

One way to bring clarity to a purpose statement includes considering what the policy will not address. An authorship policy might delineate rules around copyrightable contribution, author order, and publication readiness, but it probably would not cover any agreements surrounding collaboration or material sharing, for example. Those might get spelled out through separate documentation and not a stand-alone authorship policy. While a policy can combine related purposes (i.e., authorship + publication readiness), it typically stays contained within one major topic area.

Another way of creating a clear policy statement centers on what to name the policy. Often, giving something a title brings focus to the document, but it can also be difficult to start first with the name before conversation or drafting has occurred about the body of the document. Having a general topic in mind as a potential policy title will be sufficient to begin outreach to individuals for collaboration or conversation. As the policy purpose gets developed, the title of the policy can also get refined as part of the iterative process.

A final way of creating clarity includes being observant and aware of any repetitive issues within a research group, institution, or scholarly communication venue. If questions often get asked about a certain topic and the only answer becomes to ask other people, the question itself probably represents a potential policy solution. Keeping track of the types of questions those in

Table 4.1. Resources for Finding Policy Peers

Resources to Locate Research Policy Peers	Websites
Society of Research Administrators International	https://www.srainternational.org/
National Council of University Research Administrators	https://www.ncura.edu/
Association of College & University Policy Administrators	https://acupa.org/
Society for Scholarly Publishing	https://www.sspnet.org/
Council of Scientific Editors	https://www.councilscienceeditors.org/
American Council of Learned Societies	https://www.acls.org/
Association of University Presses	https://aupresses.org/
Committee on Publication Ethics	https://publicationethics.org/
Open Access Scholarly Publishing Association	https://oaspa.org/

similar work settings have had can help an author-as-convener, research administrator, editor, or publisher know what type of policy solution would be most beneficial. Discovering the types of questions authors and research group participants have happens organically and certainly takes time. Knowing that an author-as-convener, administrator, or editor might need to craft these policies will also become part of the ongoing policy-writing process. Setting clear position descriptions, job duties, or professional expectations also becomes an important element, but when those might be missing, utilizing other code of conduct documentation, such as research handbooks, can assist in steering authors-as-conveners in the direction of creating clear policies.

FORM A DIVERSE WORKING GROUP

With an informed purpose statement in hand, form a group to consult with on crafting wording for the policy itself. A general good practice when forming diverse working groups is to make a concerted effort to select those who might not look or think like the convener or might not share the convener's personal characteristics such as gender, race, language, sexuality, or gender expression. This would also include colleagues who are not in the same rank or administrative status as the convener. Consider including those who would be directly impacted by the policy, whether it be an institutional policy, small research group policy, or a publisher policy.

If you are a research convener, ask those within your research group: postdoctoral scholars, graduate students, undergraduate students, other faculty and staff peers. As a research administrator, bring in those from appropriate representative areas of the institution and consider employees in non-administrative positions to establish more diverse and wide-ranging perspectives. For publishers, editors, and scholarly communication event hosts, consult with authors you have worked with in the past and consider establishing a small focus group of authors across various types of institutions and types of authors (student authors, faculty authors, independent researchers, etc.). Within an author focus group convened by a publisher or scholarly communication venue, consider diversity not only in terms of life stage of authors, but also authors' gender, race, sexuality, gender expression, and first and second languages.

Next, bring in policy-writing experts, if possible. Some research universities will also have policy administrators or representatives who can assist in the policy writing and approval process. People in these types of positions can provide tremendous help and resources in policy drafting, even for those simply developing a local research group policy. Look through your institution's web pages to determine if you have a general policy director or policy liaison or consult the Association of College and University Policy Administrators. Also, while not a standard position, many academic institutions have librarians that specialize in policy work, so it can also be of benefit to reach out to your academic library to inquire about specialization. Many academic libraries also employ scholarly communication librarians, which, if you seek to develop an authorship or publishing policy, will be able to provide in-depth knowledge about the publishing and scholarly communication industry.

Share the policy purpose and other background information with the working group to initiate discussion about the best policy wording. Ask questions regarding the clarity of the purpose statement as well as its relevance. Provide the background and context by which you came to the purpose statement—that is, did you talk primarily with peer research managers or did you base it more on the types of questions that you received as convener of the research group.

As the working group comes together, take the opportunity to bring everyone on similar standing by allowing the group to collectively inform themselves on broader and related policies. When working on an authorship or publication policy, other applicable policies will include data and intellectual property ownership, codes of conduct, and academic freedom.

UNDERSTANDING THE BROADER SET OF RELATED POLICIES

Part of the role as research convener consists of providing good information and direction to the research group. Same goes for a research administrator or publishing entity seeking to organize a policy-writing group. To that end, conveners will need to familiarize themselves with the broader policies of an institution as well as the broader practices of a discipline or scholarly network. Related policies will include ownership and reuse of data, patent ownership, codes of conduct, and academic freedom. Copyright ownership policies will be central, which chapter 2 covered in detail.

Policies on data, patents, and academic freedom often exist as separate policies. Research handbooks represent one potential area to seek out details on data ownership within an academic institution. Institutional research handbooks will also include information about the roles and responsibilities of a research manager, such as safeguarding data generated through the work of a small research group but owned by the larger institution, protecting any patentable intellectual property (i.e., inventions), and ensuring the academic freedom of those participating in the research group.

Data ownership can become relevant within copyright ownership policies when also considered works of authorship, but often data alone do not meet the definition of a work of authorship. This distinction helps explain why data ownership gets spelled out in other policy areas. Most research universities claim ownership to data, especially data recorded in lab or research notebooks. This might not get promulgated through a policy labeled "data ownership" so authors-as-conveners will need to be creative in their search for these broader and related policies.

Research administrators will have had a role in establishing data ownership principles so authors-as-conveners can work closely with them on fully understanding the finer details. For research administrators seeking to establish data ownership principles through a policy, you would want to include in-house intellectual property attorneys as part of your working group. For publishers, editors, and other scholarly communication venue hosts, knowing the general landscape of data ownership practices in research universities will greatly assist with your policy-crafting process. This book will provide a few examples, but including research administrator representatives as consultants for your policy drafting could prove beneficial. Consulting with intellectual property attorneys could also be useful.

Patent ownership policies will be another related policy for authors-as-conveners to become familiar with, especially if the research is federally funded and intends to result in inventions. Most American research universities updated their patent policies after Congress passed the Bayh-Dole Act in 1980 and updated practices after the 2011 U.S. Supreme Court decision in Stanford v. Roche.[1] Inventions are distinct from copyrightable works of authorship within U.S. federal law, which is why most academic institutions will maintain separate policies for each.

Policies on academic freedom will also stand separate from any data ownership, copyright ownership or patent ownership policies. Most academic freedom rights and responsibilities will get delineated within employee and student codes of conduct. There could be additional parameters included in institutional research handbooks as well.

The primary factors of academic freedom for authors-as-conveners, research administrators, publishers, and editors to become familiar with and to guide policy working groups include the following:

Right to examine ideas
Right to communicate ideas
Right to publish the results of research

The relationship between academic freedom, authorship, and copyright ownership is close and intertwined, as detailed in chapter 2. The principles of academic freedom serve as an underpinning and foundation to any authorship or publication policy. The nuances of copyright ownership influence both authorship and academic freedom. Table 4.2 lists additional resources about academic freedom.

As we saw in chapter 2, co-authors of a copyrightable work can act upon the exclusive rights of copyright, meaning each author can participate in decisions regarding the copying, distribution, display, performance, transmission, and adaptation of a work. When an academic author-as-convener includes someone as an author on a work of scholarly authorship, that person also has a say in the work. The finer point when it comes to authorship is that one must have made a copyrightable contribution. As we saw in chapter 3, the act of "gifting" authorship for those who have not made a copyrightable contribution has been on the rise, which has necessitated a call for authorship policies within academic institutions, research groups, publishing companies, and journals. A research manager will want an authorship policy to include the copyrightable contribution aspect of authorship in order to avoid any unintentional gifting of authorship.

The same policy solution would need to be in place so that research managers do not deny authorship when a member of a research group has made a copyrightable contribution. Being clear on what "copyrightable contribution" means in context of the research group and within the policy-writing working group becomes crucial. An author-as-convener will need to educate themselves and also assist those within their working groups in obtaining a more complete understanding of these subtle connections between academic freedom, authorship, and copyright ownership.

Put simply, a copyrightable contribution extends to a member of a research group who fixes in a tangible medium an original expression of an idea. This could happen through writing or typing out the original research inquiry or describing through writing or images the result of an original research inquiry. But what does not count as a copyrightable contribution is mentoring a researcher, funding a researcher, or offering support to a researcher. These types of activities are necessary components to ensure high-quality research and productive researchers, but they do not represent copyrightable contributions. Authors-as-conveners, research administrators, publishers, and scholarly communication venues at the very least need to have this level of familiarity with copyright ownership and authorship.

Another area that authors-as-conveners, research administrators, publishers, and scholarly communication venues will need to have some awareness of is scholarly codes of conduct and academic freedom. Student and employee codes of conduct will detail elements of academic freedom and they will also include rules surrounding plagiarism and research integrity. Plagiarism typically gets defined as the intentional act of copying another's ideas, words, or process without attribution or citation. It is an academic standard (as opposed to a legality) that often also becomes an authorship question. As such, referencing the institution's definition of plagiarism within the authorship policy of a research group will be beneficial. Plagiarism is part of the larger definition of research misconduct. The two other areas of misconduct include falsification and fabrication. Codes of conduct and/or institutional research handbooks will include details on these prohibitions and referencing them in an authorship or publication policy will be important.

For publishers or scholarly communication venues seeking to incorporate appropriate code of conduct wording related to academic freedom, they could

Table 4.2. Good Resources about Academic Freedom

Books and Professional Organizations about Academic Freedom
Understanding Academic Freedom by Henry Reichman
Academic Freedom and the Inclusive University by Sharon E. Kahn and Dennis Pavlich
American Association of University Professors, https://www.aaup.org/our-work/protecting-academic-freedom
American Library Association, https://www.ala.org/advocacy/intfreedom/academicfreedom

look to professional organizations such as the American Association of University Professors and the American Library Association. One simple approach for publishers and venues to address academic freedom rights is to consider asking authors if all those who participated in the gathering of research data and everyone who made a copyrightable contribution have been included on the list of authors. The goal of such a policy or best practice would be to ensure that no one who had a right to authorship was denied authorship. It could also simply be considered a research integrity or anti-plagiarism policy.

CRAFT AN OUTLINE; USE PLAIN LANGUAGE

With a working group in place and some familiarity with surrounding policies, the work of writing the policy can begin. As with all writing projects, creating an outline will help organize the writing and keep the writing process moving forward. A sample outline to follow could include:

I. Policy Name
II. Policy Scope & Purpose
III. Definitions
IV. Policy
V. Exceptions
VI. References to Related Policies
VII. Contact for Questions

The policy can be as short or as long as needed. For an author-as-convener, the policy detailing rules of the research group will probably be shorter in length. For a research administrator, a publisher/editor, or a scholarly communication venue, the policy wording will be much longer in length in order to provide details for multiple people at an institution, multiple participants at a scholarly communication event, or multiple contributors to a scholarly journal.

One important aspect to keep in mind is utilizing plain language as much as possible. This is where knowledge of the related policies will become important. The more the language of the small research group's policy reflects similar wording from broader or related policies of the institution, the easier it will be for all participants to fully understand. It will also establish more consistent communication with the use of similar wording. The style of wording to use for a research administrator or publisher-convened group would be plain English as much as possible with the potential for publisher policies to also consider bi- or tri-lingual translations of the policy. If one exists, following an in-house style guide will be important. If one does not exist, consult good policy-writing guide books as listed in table 4.3.

Table 4.3. List of Books about Policy Writing

Books on Policy Writing
Writing Effective Policies and Procedures: A Step-by-Step Resource for Clear Communication by Nancy Campbell
Writing Public Policy: A Practical Guide to Communicating in the Policy Making Process by Catherine F. Smith
Create Your Own Employee Handbook: A Legal & Practical Guide for Employers by Lisa Guerin

In the next chapter, we will look more in depth at ways of ensuring equity and inclusion within the policy-crafting process.

NOTE

1. Lisa Lapin. "Stanford 'Disappointed' in Supreme Court Ruling in Roche Case." *Stanford Report* (June 7, 2011), https://news.stanford.edu/news/2011/june/court-roche -ruling-060711.html.

5

Equity, Diversity, and Inclusion within Policies

Policies reflect the attitudes and knowledge of an institution as well as those who write them. Worldviews, informed opinions, and personal experiences all make their way into policy documents. Despite the common understanding that policies can feel stifling, and sometimes irrelevant to the human experience (especially that of a workplace), they are a human-centered process. People write them, others tweak or edit them, and everyone makes their best effort to be guided by them.

Policies influence people, our behaviors, and actions. They also promote transparency. They provide initial instruction on procedures and processes and offer clarity when moments of uncertainty or confusion arise. Taking the time to consider in advance how one might want a procedure or process to go means that more thorough decision-making can come to the fore and also means that those within a working group can have a better idea of expectations. Equitable policies help everyone interact from a similar standing by reducing bias, discrimination, and barriers to entry.

Developing holistic policies with a broad and deep understanding of what the policy itself will represent and the type of people it will impact becomes crucial. In this chapter, we will explore more in depth the relevance of authorship, copyright ownership, and publication policies in terms of equity, diversity, and inclusion.

The topic of integrating equity, diversity, and inclusion within policies becomes important because our societies, work-life, and employment practices have a history of discrimination and also because our societies, work-life, and employment practices are changing. As we saw in chapter 3, scholarly authorship has a history that includes unfair and biased treatment, including racism, sexism, and rankism. Our workplaces are also changing, mostly driven by globalization of workforces, according to sociologist Maureen Baker.[1] With global workforces come new political realities such as managerialism, neoliberalism, and reactions to both. Academic authors and research administrators are not immune to these new realities. Sociologist Floyd W. Hayes describes higher education workforces as a "knowledge-intensive managerial society"[2] that has at the heart of it what social activist Andrew Ross refers to as "the copyfight over intellectual property."[3] Acknowledging and becoming familiar with these new realities will become important when crafting new scholarly communication policies or revising existing ones.

First, we will look at equity, diversity, and inclusion within copyright ownership policies from the perspective of research administrators and publishers. Then we will move into equity, diversity, and inclusion within authorship policies from several perspectives: research administrators, research managers, and publishers. Some good definitions of equity, diversity, and inclusion come from the Coalition for Diversity & Inclusion in Scholarly Communications. Figure 5.1 shows the working definitions they have utilized to inform their statement of principles.

Definitions

C4DISC Coalition for Diversity & Inclusion in Scholarly Communications

Accessibility enables everyone—whether or not they have a disability—to acquire the same information, engage in the same interactions, and enjoy the same services in an equally integrated and equally effective manner. Organizations shall take appropriate measures to ensure access, on an equal basis with others, to the physical environment, to transportation, to information and communications, including information and communications technologies and systems, and to other facilities and services open or provided to all.

Diversity refers to the composition of a group of people from any number of demographic backgrounds: identities (innate and selected); the collective strength of their experiences, beliefs, values, skills, and perspectives; and the historical and ongoing ways in which these groups have been affected by structures of power. The variability in a diverse group is apparent in the characteristics we see and hear, as well as through behaviors and expressions that we encounter and experience in our workplaces and organizations. Diverse organizations are not by default inclusive.

Equity ensures that all individuals are provided the resources and support they need to access opportunities available to their peers.

Inclusion is the act of establishing philosophies, policies, practices, and procedures to ensure equitable access to opportunities and resources that support individuals in contributing to an organization's success. Through encouraging awareness of power structures, creating opportunities for those who have historically been excluded, and attempting to decenter majority culture, inclusion creates the environment and infrastructure in which diversity within organizations can exist and thrive. Inclusive organizations are by definition committed to achieving a sense of belonging for everyone at all levels.

Figure 5.1. Definition of Terms Developed by the Coalition for Diversity & Inclusion in Scholarly Communications, https://c4disc.org/principles/

COPYRIGHT OWNERSHIP POLICIES + EQUITY, DIVERSITY, AND INCLUSION

RESEARCH ADMINISTRATORS

For the most part, research administrators at higher education institutions and research institutes will help establish foundational policies such as copyright ownership. They also develop other, related intellectual property policies such as patent ownership. (This book focuses only on equitable copyright ownership policies.) These policies set the stage for the institution's general attitude toward ownership of products of the mind.

A key component for research administrators to consider is one of balance. An institution that shares no ownership with individual creators will have a more difficult time recruiting author-employees. But an institution that considers ways to share ownership will become more appealing to individual creators.

Employing and working with researcher-authors becomes an activity centered on partnership and collaboration. As we saw in earlier chapters, the level of commitment required to investigate and create can amount to feeling as if a piece of one's identity goes into the process. Knowing and understanding that type of work commitment will help research administrators setting policies to establish what I call research-friendly and author-friendly policies.

Institutions support author-employees in many ways, from office and lab space to computers and other specialized equipment. This can sometimes lead research administrators to feel the level of commitment on the part of the institution warranting full ownership of work products. It is important to keep this commitment in mind, but to not let it get in the way of developing well-rounded, inclusive, and equitable ownership policies.

Shared ownership also becomes a matter of practicality while also honoring the diversity inherent in a broad group of author-employees. For an institution to be a sole owner of works of authorship created by its employees essentially means that an entity within the institution would need to be established to exercise the rights of copyright (as we saw in chapter 2). In practice, this would mean that authors of works would need to get permission from the institution to distribute their work.

For large universities and institutions, such an office would be overwhelmed by the number of permission requests from individual employees at the institution. Moreover, for any author-employees at the institution who are part of a marginalized group, this would present a potential site of bias as well as a barrier to entry. Questions could arise such as "Does the institutional copyright ownership representative differ from my perceptible identity?" and "Does the institutional copyright ownership representative agree with my area of research and work product?"

Granting full ownership of certain works signals to author-employees and potential employees that the institution trusts those that have been hired to create products of the mind. Trust leads to stronger working relationships and leads author-employees to feel more comfortable taking risks with their ideas, lines of inquiry, and works of authorship.

SCHOLARLY PUBLISHERS

The concept of displaying author friendliness extends to publishers as well as research administrators. The unique aspect of a publishing office as compared to an institution is the level of overhead. Scholarly publishing houses have overhead and expenses, yes, but taking ownership of all of a work of authorship without the requirement of also paying for academic authors' salaries, equipment, office space, etc. could be argued as less than author friendly. Considering copyright ownership policies with equity, diversity, and inclusion in mind could lead to more shared ownership and more flexibility in distribution options and choices for authors.

If, as a publisher, it feels difficult to imagine anything other than complete ownership, consider building in consistent re-uses that researcher-authors can come to rely on, such as sharing works with colleagues, trainees, or others the author might need to regularly communicate with as part of their daily work. If the author's research and writing was funded in part by public funds, certainly consider a public access policy (this, in fact, will become a requirement for authors made by virtue of U.S. government research agencies starting in 2026).

Also like research administrators, scholarly publishing houses act in partnership with researcher-authors and their academic institutions. Publishers help academic departments ease the burden of the employment review processes many use as part of the tenure system in academia. Publishers help ensure that products get reviewed and scrutinized and, while it is not a perfect system, it saves academic departments time in reading and critiquing research results in the form of original manuscripts. It stands as a significant service provided on behalf of academic departments across the country and world. Publishers are typically outside of an institution, but they are central partners in the broad scholarly communication landscape.

As publishers begin to think of themselves more as partners and collaborators in the scholarly communication system (as opposed to simply thinking of themselves as stand-alone companies, which they are, competing for works in an open marketplace), the policies could come to reflect the reality of that symbiotic relationship. In turn, author-employees can operate in a more equitable landscape that supports their goals to develop new lines of inquiry, novel methodologies, and more diverse audiences.

AUTHORSHIP POLICIES + EQUITY, DIVERSITY, AND INCLUSION

RESEARCH ADMINISTRATORS

Research administrators will want an authorship policy in order to encourage all the research units in an institution to develop one. A policy about having a policy is essentially what this would become. Such a policy helps signal that having accurate authorship remains crucial for the research enterprise. It would require research managers and academic units to take the time to define what it means to be an author, how authors should be listed on a work of authorship jointly created and know when to not include someone as an author, but instead as a contributor.

We will focus more on sample wording in the next chapter, but possible wording regarding a reference to or definition of authors in terms of equity, diversity, and inclusion could be incorporated, for example, that legitimate authors may not be excluded from a local authorship policy or that gifting of authorship is not allowed within local authorship policies. While this would not directly address any issues of discrimination or equity, it would provide appropriate guidance to those writing a department or lab policy.

Research administrators writing an institution-wide authorship policy could also take the opportunity to determine if level of contribution to a research design or line of inquiry warrants authorship. This component of authorship typically goes beyond the standard definition of authorship, which is primarily making a copyrightable contribution. Administrators would want to consult with the researcher-authors in their institution and also consider best practices, which the next chapter will focus on.

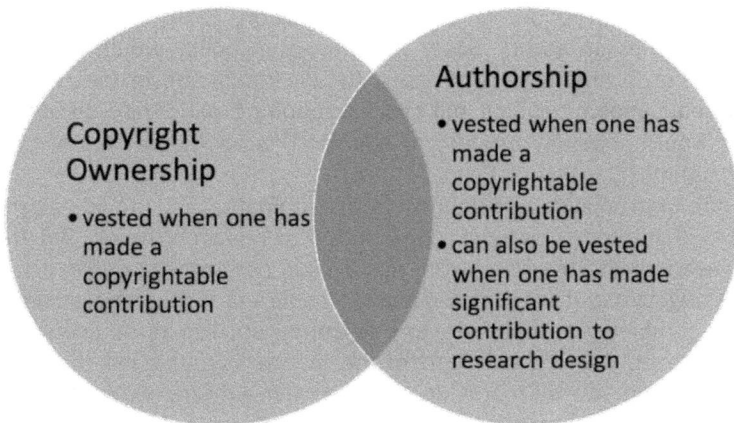

Figure 5.2. How Copyright Ownership and Authorship Intersect; Authorship Has an Additional Definition, Which Centers on When One Makes a Significant, but Non-copyrightable Contribution to the Design of a Research Project

RESEARCH OR LAB MANAGERS

For research managers, accuracy in authorship listing is very important. Knowing the rules about what constitutes authorship will become a mainstay of any local authorship policies. The basic definition as we have seen throughout this book is that an author is someone who makes a copyrightable contribution to a work. For a contribution to be considered copyrightable, a person needs to have fixed an original expression of an idea into a tangible medium. These terms and definitions will reside in the institution's copyright ownership policy. Research managers would incorporate these concepts into their daily thinking and practice as well as their authorship policy.

A research manager has the difficult task of overseeing all research and publishing decision-making, but the one area where a manager does not necessarily make an independent decision is the rules of authorship. If, as a manager, a researcher-author does not want to include someone on a work as a co-author, then the manager would not include that person in the overall research project. The publication policy would reflect the manager's inclination or preference on author order (i.e., alphabetical listing vs. ordering based on level of contribution and supervision), but neither an authorship nor a publication policy would include a personal preference about what counts as authorship vis-à-vis copyrightable contribution. That, again, would be spelled out in the institution's copyright ownership policy. If the institution's policy allows for contribution to research design as a measure of authorship, then the research manager would have some leeway on personal preference regarding inclusive authorship.

Having a local lab policy will help alleviate any potential discrimination within authorship determination. If someone in the lab or research group has made a copyrightable contribution—no matter the gender, race, sexual orientation, gender expression, veteran status, religion, ability, or ethnicity—that person becomes an author. Sadly, an authorship policy would not preclude a research or lab manager from potential discrimination in the selection or hiring of educational trainees, but the institution's broader non-discrimination policies would hopefully attempt to address this additional area of potential discrimination.

Authorship policies help define non-discrimination and provide a definition of what constitutes substantial contribution to research design. But they do not always indicate the role of the manager in determining publication decision-making. Without seeming too heavy on policies, a research manager could consider combining authorship and publication policies as outlined in Figure 5.1 into a single document as part of the research group's handbook of best practices. Doing so would provide all researcher-authors within the group an easily accessible document detailing these procedures. Such a handbook could also become an opportunity to communicate a commitment to and interest in equity, diversity, and inclusion. Table 5.1 shows potential elements of authorship and copyright ownership that research managers could utilize.

Table 5.1. Distinguishing Features of Authorship and Publication Policies within a Lab or Research Group

Differences Between Authorship and Publication Policies within a Research Group	
Authorship Policy	*Publication Policy*
• Applying non-discrimination statement from institutional policy in authorship determinations • Incorporating definition of copyright ownership and copyrightable contribution from institutional policy • If applicable, discussing how significant contribution to research design will be determined if no copyrightable contribution is present • Agreement for all co-authors to be accountable for "all aspects of the work"[a]	• Role of research manager or convener in determining readiness of data for publication • Guidance on how publication venues get selected and how research team members can participate in the selection of publication venue • Delineation of roles and responsibilities for manuscript submission, the general practice on determination of author order, and other publication-related matters such as self-archiving, data management, and public access requirements

[a] This phrasing and the recommendation to utilize an agreement comes from the *International Committee for Medical Journal Editors' Defining the Role of Authors and Contributors.*

SCHOLARLY PUBLISHERS

A publisher's authorship policy would be similar to an institutional authorship policy created by a research administrator. The goal would be to indicate that the publishing company expects accuracy in authorship. When requiring accuracy in authorship, practices of individual publication outlets would get influenced. For example, on a submission form for a publication venue, the workflow would require wording asking authors to confirm or warrant that all those who made a copyrightable contribution to the work are reflected on the authorship list. Based on the policy, the form could also ask those submitting to confirm or warrant that only those who made a copyrightable contribution to the work are listed as authors (i.e., no "gifting" of authorship).

While the terms "equity," "diversity," "inclusion" might not expressly be utilized in a publisher policy or as part of the submission workflow, the fact that the policy and workflow asks for submitters to warrant inclusion of all authors will help address any inadvertent (or deliberate) exclusionary, unfair, or discriminatory actions on the part of researcher-authors.

In the next two chapters, we will look more closely at existing, sample copyright ownership and authorship policies.

NOTES

1. Maureen Baker. *Restructuring Family Policies: Convergences and Divergences* (Toronto: University of Toronto Press, 2006), *ProQuest Ebook Central*, https://ebookcentral .proquest.com/lib/utah/detail.action?docID=4671904.
2. Floyd W. Hayes. *Politics of Knowledge: Black Policy Professionals in the Managerial Age*. In *A Companion to African-American Studies*, edited by Jane Anna Gordon and Lewis Gordon (Hoboken, NJ: John Wiley & Sons, 2006), *ProQuest Ebook Central*, https:// ebookcentral.proquest.com/lib/utah/detail.action?docID=255303.
3. Andrew Ross. *Nice Work if You Can Get It: Life and Labor in Precarious Times* (New York: New York University Press, 2009), *ProQuest Ebook Central*, https://ebook central.proquest.com/lib/utah/detail.action?docID=865907.

6

Sample Copyright Ownership Policies

In this chapter, we will look more in depth into the elements of copyright ownership by examining sample policies from three different institutions: California Institute of the Arts (CalArts), the University of Texas System (UT System), and the University of Chicago Press. All of the sample policies represent examples of accuracy and fairness in approaches to copyright ownership as well as clarity in reuse for academic authors.

As we have seen in previous chapters, a copyright ownership policy presents an opportunity to consider equity and inclusion within an institution. Equity becomes relevant in terms of part ownership in intellectual property—a shared partnership between academic author and institution. In an equitable scenario, neither one receives full ownership. Instead, the policy becomes the mechanism by which the institution indicates shared ownership.

When academic authors receive equity by means of the works they create as employees, it generates opportunities for both remuneration and decision-making authority. An equitable copyright ownership policy also has the chance to be inclusive of employees at an institution, making the endeavor of research and creativity more than simply an administrative or institution-owned effort. In essence, an equitable copyright ownership policy establishes the autonomy and independence necessary for an inclusive workplace where employees have ownership interest in the institution as well as an environment that fosters free and open thought and communication.

Honoring institutional commitment is important with regard to creation of intellectual property, and as these sample policies will show, it remains possible to present the nuances of when the institution needs to take a broader ownership interest and when individual creators, artists, and authors need more individual or sole ownership interest. The example from CalArts shows this nuance very well in a succinct and straightforward manner.

The sample policy from the UT System also shows distinctions between individual and institutional ownership but does so more from the perspective of institution-based research partnerships and commercialization interests.

The result is the same, however, because the policy establishes equity and is inclusive of employees. The University of Chicago Press's policy provides an example of utmost clarity in detailing how academic authors can engage in reusing the works they have created as a shared interest, in this case, between publishers and authors.

CALIFORNIA INSTITUTE OF THE ARTS

As an art and design school, the CalArts has a unique and innovative copyright ownership policy that honors the role of the individual author and artist in maintaining as much control and ownership as possible over works of authorship. It is one of the few policies that uses the term "sale" in its name: "Policy on Ownership, Copyright, and Sale of Objects of Art Created by Members of the Institute." Also unique is the immediate reference to equity within the policy's opening line: "to encourage every member to realize the maximum economic potential from the works he/she creates while a member of the Institute."[1] Figure 6.1 shows this line within the context of the opening statement of the policy along with the details of how the policy helps CalArts achieve their stated goal by distinguishing between differing types of creative efforts: one describing works commissioned by CalArts, another for grant-based or other subsidized works, and a third describing ownership of independent and individual works. The categorization helps establish clarity in the section detailing ownership.

Policies

Revised Policies

New Policies

Policies Under Review

All Policies

ALL

ACADEMIC

CATALOG

EMPLOYMENT
& WORKPLACE

FACULTY
AFFAIRS

FINANCIAL
MANAGEMENT

INSTITUTE
AFFAIRS

SAFETY &
SECURITY

STUDENT LIFE

CALARTS
PRIVACY
POLICY

DATA
RETENTION
POLICY

Print All
Policies

Institute Affairs: Policy on Ownership, Copyright and Sale of Objects of Art Created by Members of the Institute

It is the policy of the California Institute of the Arts to encourage every member to realize the maximum economic potential from the works he/she creates while a member of the Institute. To this end all copyrights and patents to such works are to remain in the name of their creator. It is suggested that the creator take necessary steps to perfect and preserve these rights. At the same time the creative efforts of students and faculty play a significant role in the learning experience. Therefore, the Institute reserves the right to retain a copy of members' creations which are to be used solely for non-commercial educational purposes.

The following observations should assist in explaining the foregoing policy.

A. Three Categories of Creative Effort
Students and faculty members have all rights to their work and all editorial control, except as specifically modified by agreements made at the creator's discretion. The degree of modification may be described by three categories in which various arrangements for funding and editorial control can be made.

1. Institute Commissioned Work
If a person or group within the Institute, that has the authority, The Institute has ownership of any work that it commissions, including the right to use or not to use, as it determines. If the Institute rejects a project it has commissioned it retains ownership and control.

(continued)

Figure 6.1. Shows a Portion of CalArt's Policy on Copyright Ownership

The Institute has ownership of any work that it commissions, including the right to use or not to use, as it determines. If the Institute rejects a project it has commissioned it retains ownership and control.

2. Subsidized Work
In subsidized work the relationship between the subsidizer and the creative person is one of mutual agreement, wherein the limitations or terms of control are made prior to the execution of the project. The range of editorial control that the subsidizer acquires is granted at the discretion of the creator who will be doing the work. However, as to external subsidies the Institute retains the right to approve and to participate, if it desires, in the contractual arrangements. If the Institute refuses to approve an external subsidy the student or faculty member is free to arrange it on an individual basis; but no Institute materials or facilities may be used, and the Institute official imprint, or credit, may not be attached to the work.

3. Independent Work
Independent work is completely within the control of the individual student or group. This is the general condition under which students and faculty work, except when arrangements have been made that fall under one of the above classifications.

Anything provided to the enrolled student, such as basic materials that are normal to his/her course of instruction, is not to be considered a form of subsidy. Enrollment at CalArts grants the right to use certain supplies and the right to use facilities in the production of creative work over which the student retains all control.

It is advantageous to the Institute to have faculty members actively producing creative work on campus rather than elsewhere. This enhances their position with the public as well as with the students; and when possible the facilities of the different Schools should be extended to them.

B. Ownership and Patent Rights
When work is done under the classification of independent work the student or faculty member retains all rights to the work. Work done under the classification of subsidized or commissioned work is subject to modification of the ownership or patent rights under the terms of the contract agreements made before the work is begun

Figure 6.1. *(continued)*

THE UNIVERSITY OF TEXAS SYSTEM

Similar to CalArts, the UT System utilizes its policy on copyright ownership to convey the importance of economic development. But unlike CalArts, the domain of the UT System policy extends beyond an individual artist or creator and instead anticipates a system-wide and multi-institutional impact within the private sector. The UT System policy represents a much broader range of types of institutions and works of authorship and establishes a more detailed level of shared ownership and equity. Figure 6.2 shows the full policy for the UT System. Through the policy, academic authors (a distinct category separate from students) assign rights to the UT System Board of Regents. The policy provides for the carve out mentioned in earlier chapters that allows academic authors to retain copyright in traditional scholarly works in order to engage in the scholarly communication system. This creates the conditions for equity as well as academic freedom.

The University of Texas System
Rules and Regulations of the Board of Regents   **Rule: 90101**

1.   **Title**

        Intellectual Property

2.   **Rule and Regulation**

        Sec. 1   Preamble. This intellectual property Rule is intended to serve the public good, promote partnerships with the private sector, encourage innovation, promote the engagement of faculty, staff, and students in research, and foster economic development. The Board of Regents recognizes the high importance of discovery commercialization as a core mission. U. T. System recognizes that it will attract more collaborative research supported by industry if timely and efficient processes exist to manage intellectual property.

        This Rule is intended to be adaptable to the highly varied circumstances that characterize the private sector and the portfolio of research at U. T. System institutions. In all cases, U. T. System institutions will strive to enable the ease of intellectual property creation, protection, management, and transfer to the private sector and society within an environment that promotes the highest quality and integrity of academic activity, teaching, and research.

        U. T. System is guided by the following fundamental principles on intellectual property:

(continued)

Figure 6.2. The University of Texas System Rules and Regulations of the Board of Regents. Intellectual Property.

1.1   The successful deployment of intellectual property developed through teaching, research, discovery, creative activities, and application of knowledge, whether through sponsored research, licensing, or other types of transactions or arrangements, allows for knowledge and technology to be disseminated to benefit the broad public and comports with the mission of the U. T. System;

1.2   Sponsored research is very important to the vitality and competitiveness of U. T. System institutions, the State of Texas, and our nation. All U. T. System institutions shall (a) encourage and strengthen university-industry partnerships, (b) efficiently and expeditiously manage intellectual property created from these partnerships, and (c) remain understanding, flexible, and open to the varied circumstances and needs of potential industry sponsors;

1.3   U. T. System institutions should expect that when industry is underwriting sponsored research, industry commences negotiations with the expectation of speed in the execution of critical agreements, clear financial outcomes, and ownership rights in, or appropriate access to, intellectual property resulting from the work;

1.4   Sponsored research is frequently tightly integrated with the educational mission at many U. T. System institutions but must not abridge publication and research rights, impinge upon the dissemination of research results, including student theses and dissertations, nor diminish an environment of academic and research integrity;

1.5   The primary research-related duties of members of the faculty at U. T. System institutions are to teach, study, investigate, discover, create, disseminate, develop professionally, and infuse new knowledge into their classes and student interaction;

1.6   Commercialization of technology enhances the reputation of the U. T. System and enables transformation of knowledge into the marketplace; and

1.7   Compliance with all applicable federal laws and regulations, the Texas Constitution, and applicable laws of the State of Texas is essential for successful U. T. System technology commercialization.

Sec. 2   Ownership of Intellectual Property. Except as set forth in Section 5, the Board of Regents automatically owns the intellectual property created by individuals subject to this Rule, yet recognizes the importance of discovery commercialization. In appropriate circumstances concerning intellectual property resulting from research supported by (a) an entirely private, nongovernmental grant or contract with a nonprofit or for-profit entity, or (b) an entirely private gift or grant to the U. T. System

Figure 6.2. *(continued)*

or any U. T. System institution, as set forth in Section 12.1, the U. T. System or a U. T. System institution may enter into an agreement to transfer or grant appropriate access to the Board of Regents' rights in intellectual property to third parties. For purposes of this Rule, intellectual property includes, but is not limited to, any invention, discovery, creation, know-how, trade secret, technology, scientific or technological development, research data, work of authorship and software, regardless of whether subject to protection under patent, trademark, copyright, or other laws.

Sec. 3   Individuals Subject to this Rule. While students are governed by Section 6, this Rule applies to all persons employed by the U. T. System or any U. T. System institution, as well as to anyone using the facilities or resources of the U. T. System or any U. T. System institution. All individuals subject to this Rule must assign, and do hereby assign, their rights in such intellectual property to the Board of Regents, and such individuals shall promptly execute and deliver all documents and other instruments as are reasonably necessary to reflect the Board of Regents' ownership of such intellectual property. A creator of intellectual property owned by the Board of Regents has no independent right or authority to convey, assign, encumber, or license such intellectual property other than to the Board of Regents. U. T. System institutions may promulgate institutional rules, regulations, or policies defining the course and scope of employment for persons or classes of persons and specifying that authorized outside employment is or is not within an employee's course and scope of employment.

Sec. 4   Intellectual Property Subject to this Rule. Intellectual property (a) developed within the course and scope of employment of the individual, (b) resulting from activities performed on U. T. System time or with support of state funds, or (c) resulting from using facilities or resources owned by the U. T. System or any U. T. System institution (other than incidental use) is owned by the Board of Regents.

Sec. 5   Intellectual Property Not Subject to this Rule. Intellectual property developed or created by a U. T. System employee outside the course and scope of employment of the individual that is developed or created on his/her own time and without the support of the U. T. System or any U. T. System institution or use of U. T. System facilities or resources, is the exclusive property of the creator.

Sec. 6   Students and Intellectual Property. A student enrolled at a U. T. System institution, such as in an undergraduate or graduate degree program or certificate program, including a postdoctoral and predoctoral fellow, owns the intellectual property he or she creates (a) in courses, (b) during extracurricular activities, and institutions commonly provided for a student's use and for which a student has paid tuition and fees, unless:

(continued)

Figure 6.2.   *(continued)*

Sample Copyright Ownership Policies   **55**

6.1   The student is also an employee of the U. T. System or any U. T. System institution and the intellectual property is developed within the course and scope of his or her employment, in which case the provisions of this Rule relating to employees shall apply;

6.2   The student works on a work-for-hire or institutional project as described by Section 8, in which case Section 8 governs that work;

6.3   The student participates in a research project where any intellectual property created under that project has already been committed to, or encumbered by an agreement with, a governmental, philanthropic, corporate or other sponsor, including a sponsor as described in Section 12.1; or

6.4   The student jointly creates the intellectual property with a non-student, in which case this Rule (other than Section 6) and applicable law dictate ownership of the intellectual property as if the student was a non-student described in Section 3.

Sec. 7   Interest in Certain Copyrights. Notwithstanding Section 2 but subject to Section 12, the Board of Regents will not assert an ownership interest in the copyright of scholarly or educational materials, artworks, musical compositions, and literary works related to the author's academic or professional field, regardless of the medium of expression. Such creators are encouraged to manage their copyrights in accordance with the guidelines concerning management and marketing of copyrighted works consistent with applicable institutional policies.

As the Board of Regents has done historically, as reasonably required for the limited purpose of continuing an institution's scheduled course offerings, the Board of Regents retains for one year following the loss of a course instructor's services a fully paid-up, royalty-free, nonexclusive worldwide license to use, copy, distribute, display, perform, and create derivative works of materials prepared by the instructor (including lectures, lecture notes, syllabi, study guides, bibliographies, visual aids, images, diagrams, multimedia presentations, examinations, web-ready content, and educational software) for use in teaching a course.

Sec. 8   Works for Hire and Institutional Projects. Notwithstanding any provisions of Sections 6 or 7 to the contrary, the Board of Regents shall have sole ownership of all intellectual property created by (a) an employee, student, or other individual or entity commissioned, required, authorized, or hired specifically to produce such intellectual property by the U. T. System or any U. T. System institution, and (b) an employee, student, or other individual as part of an institutional project. The provisions of Section 11.5 shall not apply to intellectual property governed by

Figure 6.2.   *(continued)*

this Section unless approved by the institution or U. T. System Administration in a written agreement.

Sec. 9   Use of Research Data. Research data or results created by an employee are owned by the Board of Regents and except to the extent that rights to such research data are contractually assigned or licensed to another by the Board of Regents, the creator shall have a nonexclusive license to use such data for patient care, teaching, scholarly, and other academically related purposes and nonprofit research, provided such activities are within the scope of the employee's employment.

Sec. 10   Use of Facilities and Resources. Other than in connection with student-owned intellectual property governed by Section 6, U. T. System and U. T. System institution facilities and resources may not be used (a) to create, develop, or commercialize intellectual property outside the course and scope of employment of an individual, or (b) to further develop or commercialize intellectual properties that have been released to an inventor by the Board of Regents under Section 11.2, except as the institution's president may approve in writing where the U. T. System retains an interest under the terms of the release.

Sec. 11   Invention Disclosure and Commercialization.

11.1   Determination of the Board of Regents' Interest. Before intellectual property owned by the Board of Regents is disclosed to any party outside the U. T. System, to the public generally, or for commercial purposes, and before publishing same, the creator shall submit a reasonably complete and detailed invention disclosure of such intellectual property to the president (or designee) of his or her institution for determination of the Board of Regents' interest. The institution will regularly and promptly communicate with the creator during this decision-making process and commercialization shall not proceed until that decision is made.

11.2   Election Not to Assert Ownership Interest. If the institution's president elects not to assert the Board of Regents' ownership interest, the institution's president shall notify the U. T. System Office of General Counsel and the primary creator in writing within 20 business days after the decision is made that the institution will release the intellectual property to the creator, except where prohibited by law or contractual obligations or requirements. Thereafter, the creator will be free to obtain and exploit a patent or other intellectual property protection in his or her own right and the U. T. System and U. T. System institutions shall not have any further rights, obligations, or duties with respect thereto except that, in appropriate circumstances, the institution's president may elect to (a) retain income rights, and (b) impose certain limitations or obligations, including, but

(continued)

Figure 6.2. *(continued)*

Sample Copyright Ownership Policies   **57**

not limited to, a nonexclusive license for the creator, U. T. System, and any U. T. System institution to use the released invention for patient care, teaching, scholarly, and other academically related purposes, nonprofit research, and to comply with United States government reporting and license requirements.

11.3 Later Release of Invention. Except where prohibited by law or contractual obligations or requirements, the institution's president may elect to release an invention to its creator at any time after asserting the Board of Regents' ownership interest, with notice to the U. T. System Office of General Counsel; however, such release must include provisions for the recovery by U. T. System of any patent and licensing expenses as well as the retention of income rights by U. T. System, and may include certain limitations or obligations, including those set forth in Section 11.2.

11.4 Protection and Commercialization of Intellectual Property. With respect to intellectual property in which the Board of Regents asserts an interest, the institution's president, or his or her designee, shall decide how, when, and where the intellectual property is to be protected and commercialized. The institution may contract with outside counsel for legal services with the prior consent of the Vice Chancellor and General Counsel and, if required by law, the approval of the Attorney General.

11.5 Reimbursement of Licensing Costs and Allocation of Income. In those instances where the U. T. System or any U. T. System institution licenses rights in intellectual property to third parties, the costs of licensing, including, but not limited to, the costs to operate and support a technology transfer office and the costs of obtaining a patent or other protection for the property on behalf of the Board of Regents must first be recaptured from any royalties or other license payments received by the U. T. System or any U. T. System institution. The remainder of any such income (including, but not limited to, license fees, prepaid royalties, minimum royalties, running royalties, milestone payments, and sublicense payments) shall be divided as follows:

30-50% to creator(s), and
50-70% to U. T. System institutions.

The U. T. System or the U. T. System institution shall decide on a case-by-case basis the allocation of income within these ranges for all creators, with the remainder to be disbursed to and/or retained by the U. T. System or the applicable U. T. System institution. A creator may, however, disclaim his/her interest in such income, in which case the institution shall receive and/or retain the

Figure 6.2. *(continued)*

creator's share and shall decide, in its sole discretion, if, how and when to disburse such income. Income received and/or retained by the U. T. System or any U. T. System institution from any intellectual property shall be used by the U. T. System institution where the intellectual property originated.

Sec. 12   Sponsored Research.

12.1   Private Sources. Intellectual property resulting from research supported by private sources is owned by the Board of Regents. However, with respect to intellectual property resulting from research entirely supported by (a) a private, nongovernmental grant or contract with a nonprofit or for-profit entity, or (b) a private gift or grant to the U. T. System or any U. T. System institution, if otherwise permitted by this Rule, applicable law and Section 12.3, the U. T. System and U. T. System institutions are permitted and encouraged to negotiate an agreement acceptable to U. T. System Administration or applicable U. T. System institution to transfer or grant appropriate access to the Board of Regents' ownership rights or other rights in the intellectual property resulting from such arrangements to the sponsor or the sponsor's designee. Any such agreement shall be negotiated:

(a)   In accordance with the needs and preferences of the parties, as best may be accomplished;

(b)   With flexibility and adaptability in mind;

(c)   In a timely, cooperative, and efficient manner; and

(d)   In a manner which identifies the benefits that accrue to U. T. System institutions as set forth by Section 15.2.

12.2   Public Sources. Intellectual property resulting from research supported by a grant or contract with the government (federal and/or state) or an agency thereof is owned by the Board of Regents.

12.3   Nonconformance with Intellectual Property Guidelines. Approval by a U. T. System institution under Section 15.2 of grants and contracts containing ownership and other provisions inconsistent with this Rule and other policies and guidelines adopted by the Board of Regents, including, but not limited to, The University of Texas Systemwide Policy UTS 125, *Guidance for Negotiating Research Agreements with Sponsors and Processing Research and Intellectual Property Agreements* is permissible, as it implies a decision that the benefit and value to the U. T. System or any U. T. System institution from receiving the grant or performing the contract

(continued)

Figure 6.2.   *(continued)*

Sample Copyright Ownership Policies   **59**

outweighs the impact of any nonconforming provisions on the intellectual property policies and guidelines of the U. T. System or any U. T. System institution, such as The University of Texas Systemwide Policy UTS 125, *Guidance for Negotiating Research Agreements with Sponsors and Processing Research and Intellectual Property Agreements*.

12.4   Conflicting Provisions. Subject to approval as described in Section 12.3, the intellectual property policies and guidelines of the U. T. System or any U. T. System institution are subject to, and thus amended and superseded by, the specific terms pertaining to intellectual property rights included in state and/or federal grants and contracts, or grants and contracts with nonprofit and for-profit nongovernmental entities or private donors, to the extent of any such conflict.

12.5   Cooperation with Necessary Assignments. Those persons subject to this Rule whose intellectual property creations result from (a) a grant or contract with the government (federal and/or state), or any agency thereof, (b) a grant or contract with a nonprofit or for-profit nongovernmental entity, or (c) private gift to the U. T. System or any U. T. System institution, shall promptly execute and deliver such documents and other instruments as are reasonably necessary for the U. T. System or any U. T. System institution to discharge its obligations, expressed or implied, under the particular agreement.

12.6   Sharing of Royalty Income. In the event that two or more persons who are entitled to share royalty income or equity cannot agree in writing on an appropriate sharing arrangement, the institution's president shall determine that portion of the royalty income (or equity) to which the creators are entitled under the circumstances and such amount will be distributed (or issued) to them accordingly. In the event that the creators are located at two or more U. T. System institutions and cannot agree, such royalty (or equity) distribution decision shall be made by the involved institutions' presidents (or their respective designees). In the further event that the involved presidents cannot agree, then the Chancellor shall decide and his/her decision shall be binding on the creators.

12.7   Geographical Scope of Protection. A decision by the U. T. System or any U. T. System institution to seek patent or other available protection for intellectual property covered by Section 9 shall not obligate the U. T. System or any U. T. System institution to pursue such protection in all national jurisdictions. The U. T. System's decision relating to the geographical scope and duration of such protection shall be final.

Figure 6.2.   *(continued)*

Sec. 13   Equity Interests.

    13.1   Agreements with Business Entities. The U. T. System or any U. T. System institution may receive equity interests as partial or total compensation for the conveyance of intellectual property rights. The institution where the intellectual property was created may elect, at its sole option and discretion, to share an equity interest, dividend income, or a percentage of the proceeds of the sale of an equity interest with the creator(s). The U. T. System or any U. T. System institution may also receive equity interests in a business entity as consideration for the institution's role as a founder, or for other contributions made to the business entity other than as a licensor, and the institution shall not be obligated to share such equity interests with the creator(s). The U. T. System or any U. T. System institution may also, but shall not be obligated to, negotiate an equity interest on behalf of any employee who conceived, created, discovered, invented, or developed intellectual property owned by the Board of Regents that is the subject of an agreement between the U. T. System or any U. T. System institution and a business entity relating thereto.

    13.2   Creator Holding Equity and Managing Conflict of Interest. Employees of the U. T. System Administration or any U. T. System institution who conceive, create, discover, invent, or develop intellectual property may hold an equity interest in a business entity that has an agreement with the U. T. System or any U. T. System institution relating to the research, development, licensing, or exploitation of that intellectual property only so long as the institution where the intellectual property was developed is in full compliance with the requirement to have, implement, and enforce for that employee an effective conflict of interest management plan as set forth in the U. T. System Office of General Counsel's Procedure for Managing Conflicts of Interest. In any case where an actual conflict of interest is found, the employee may be required to divest the equity interest or terminate affected research.

Sec. 14   Conflicts of Interest.

    14.1   Approval to Serve as Officer or Director. Any individual subject to Sections 2, 3, 4, or 8 who conceives, creates, discovers, invents, or develops intellectual property may serve, in his/her individual capacity, as a member of the board of directors or other governing board or as an officer or an employee (other than as a consultant) of a business entity that has an agreement with the U. T. System or any U. T. System institution relating to the research, development, licensing, or exploitation of that intellectual property only so long as the institution where

Figure 6.2.   *(continued)*

(continued)

Sample Copyright Ownership Policies   **61**

the intellectual property was developed is in full compliance with the requirement to have, implement, and enforce for that individual an effective conflict of interest management plan as set forth in the U. T. System Office of General Counsel's Procedure for Managing Conflicts of Interest. In any case where an actual conflict of interest is found, the individual may be required to terminate the business relationship or the relevant research.

14.2   Request for Employee to Serve as Officer or Director. When requested by the Board of Regents, an employee may serve on behalf of the Board of Regents as a member of the board of directors or other governing board of a business entity that has an agreement with the U. T. System or any U. T. System institution relating to the research, development, licensing, or exploitation of intellectual property, but may not accept any consideration offered for service on such board.

14.3   Report of Equity Interest and Service as Officer or Director. Any individual subject to this Rule must report in writing to the president of the institution the name of any business entity in which the person has an interest or for which the person serves as a director, officer, or employee, and shall be responsible for submitting a revised written report upon any change in the interest or position held by such person in such business entity. The U. T. System institution or its office of technology commercialization will file a report by October 1 of each year with the Office of the Board of Regents for transmittal to the Comptroller of Public Accounts as required by Section 51.912 and Section 51.005, *Texas Education Code*.

Sec. 15   Execution of Documents Related to Intellectual Property.

15.1   Execution of Agreements. Agreements that grant an interest in the Board of Regents' intellectual property, including, but not limited to, option and license agreements and contracts with corporate sponsors, may be executed and delivered in accordance with the provisions of Regents' Rule 10501, after any required review by the U. T. System Office of General Counsel.

15.2   Agreements That Do Not Conform to the Rules. Any agreement that deviates substantially from this Rule or other policies and guidelines adopted by the Board of Regents, including, but not limited to, The University of Texas Systemwide Policy UTS 125, *Guidance for Negotiating Research Agreements with Sponsors and Processing Research and Intellectual Property Agreements* may be executed and delivered as set forth above if, in the judgment of the institution's president and

Figure 6.2.   *(continued)*

after any required review by the U. T. System Office of General Counsel, the benefits from the level of funding for proposed research and/or other consideration from a sponsor, licensee, or other party outweigh any potential disadvantage that may result from the deviation.

15.3   Delegation of Authority. The Chancellor, the appropriate Executive Vice Chancellor, or the Vice Chancellor and General Counsel may execute, on behalf of the Board of Regents, legal documents relating to the Board of Regents' rights in intellectual property, including, but not limited to, assignments of ownership, applications, declarations, affidavits, powers of attorney, disclaimers, and other such documents relating to patents and copyrights; applications, declarations, affidavits, affidavits of use, powers of attorney, and other such documents relating to trademarks; and corporate documents related to the formation of new companies. In addition, the institution's president may execute, on behalf of the Board of Regents, (a) institutional applications for registration or recordation of transfers of ownership and other such documents relating to copyrights, and (b) corporate documents related to the formation of new companies (including, but not limited to, documents memorializing equity interests received under Section 13 and stockholder consents that may subsequently be sought in connection therewith), if first reviewed and approved by (i) the U. T. System Office of General Counsel, or (ii) the institution's outside counsel working under a U. T. System Office of General Counsel-approved outside counsel agreement.

3.   Definitions

None

4.   Relevant Federal and State Statutes

35 U.S.C. 18 – Patent Rights in Inventions Made with Federal Assistance (The Bayh Dole Act of 1980, as amended)

Texas Education Code Section 51.005 – Reports

Texas Education Code Section 51.912 – Equity Ownership: Business Participation

Texas Education Code, Chapter 153 – Centers for Technology Development and Transfer

5.   Relevant System Policies, Procedures and Forms

Regents' *Rules and Regulations*, Rule 10501 – Delegation to Act on Behalf of the Board of Regents

(continued)

Figure 6.2.   *(continued)*

The University of Texas Systemwide Policy UTS 125, *Guidance for Negotiating Research Agreements with Sponsors and Processing Research and Intellectual Property Agreements*

U. T. System Office of General Counsel's Procedure for Managing Conflicts of Interest

6.   **Who Should Know**

Administrators
Faculty
Staff
Students

7.   **U. T. System Administration Office(s) Responsible for Rule**

Office of General Counsel

8.   **Dates Approved or Amended**

Editorial amendment to Sec. 15.3 made September 25, 2018
Editorial amendment to Sec. 12.3, Sec. 15.2, and Number 5 made March 27, 2018
Editorial amendment to Sec. 15.3 made May 8, 2017
November 10, 2016
August 20, 2015 (Rules 90101 - Rule 90106 combined into one new Rule 90101)

9.   **Contact Information**

Questions or comments regarding this Rule should be directed to:

- bor@utsystem.edu

Figure 6.2.   *(continued)*

THE UNIVERSITY OF CHICAGO PRESS

The University of Chicago Press policy focuses on the rights of authors and provides excellent details on what the publisher permits authors to do with the works they have created. Figure 6.3 shows the full policy, but the most salient piece comes at the beginning of the policy document as it indicates the overall mission of the scholarly endeavor and how the publisher views the essential role academic authors play in furthering that mission through both teaching and publishing. Through its policy, the publisher develops shared equity for academic authors by establishing the support and foundation needed for authors to engage in additional dissemination and scholarly conversations.

YOUR RIGHTS AS AN AUTHOR

Our mission at the University of Chicago Press is to disseminate scholarship of the highest standard, to advance scholarly conversation within and across traditional disciplines, and to help define new areas of knowledge and intellectual endeavor. When you publish an article in a journal of the University of Chicago Press or one of its publishing partners, you gain the benefits of working with a professional publishing house that has over a century of commitment to the scholarly enterprise and expertise in both traditional and new electronic channels of scholarly communication. You are assured of reliable, long-term, widespread distribution of your article to a broad audience throughout the world.

We support and encourage authors' own efforts to promote and disseminate their intellectual works. As an author, you have certain rights to use your article for research, teaching, and scholarly purposes, described briefly here. For a full description of your rights, please see our Guidelines for Journal Authors' Rights.

Use for Teaching
You may use any version of your article (except proofs) for teaching purposes if you observe these conditions. There is no postpublication embargo on use of the VoR for this purpose. Allowable use includes:

- making copies for each student, either individually or as part of a printed course pack
- making the article available through print or electronic reserve or on a learning management platform

Use in Presentations
You may use any version of your article (except proofs) in oral presentations or webinars if you observe these conditions. There is no postpublication embargo on use of the VoR for this purpose. Allowable use includes:

- making copies for members of the audience
- including excerpts in shareable presentation slides

Send to Colleagues
You may provide single copies of any version of your article (except proofs) in either print or electronic form to a limited number of your colleagues for the purposes of scholarly discussion if you observe these conditions. There is no postpublication embargo on use of the VoR for this purpose.

(continued)

Figure 6.3. The University of Chicago Press—Your Rights as an Author.

Share with News Media

We encourage you to share the published results of your research with the news media. To help you get started, you may wish to view a list of our author resources. Our marketing department can help you or your institution's news office identify news sources, blogs, and other relevant outlets that may be interested in your research. Before you share your work with the news media, please review these important cautions and conditions.

Republish or Adapt Excerpts or Entire Article

You may republish your article in any subsequent book, article, or other scholarly work of which you are an author or an editor, provided that appropriate credit is given to the journal and you observe these conditions.

Deposit to a Repository or Preprint/Working Paper Service

You may deposit pre- and postacceptance versions of your article to a repository or preprint/working paper service. Your right to deposit your article in any such service is determined by the version of your article that you post and whether the service is operated in a noncommercial manner. Before you deposit your article, please review this important information about the type of service, conditions that you must observe, Creative Commons licenses, and institutional or funder mandates.

Post on Personal or Departmental Web Page

You may post any version of your article (except proofs) on your personal or departmental web page if you observe these conditions, but we strongly encourage you to post only the CAL and link to the VoR. Strong online usage statistics, which are very important for tracking readership of your paper, play a vital role in identifying where your work may be making its strongest impact—but the ability to gain such data is lost with an easily pirated PDF.

Post on Social Media Platforms

You must observe these conditions when sharing your work on commercial social media or article-sharing platforms including Facebook, Twitter, LinkedIn, Academia.edu, and ResearchGate. Except in certain limited circumstances, you may not share the VoR or AAM on such platforms.

For further information, please review these key concepts :

Manuscript version
Prior publication
Concurrent submission
Publication date
Open access or free access
Creative Commons license
Institutional or funder mandate
Repositories and preprint/working paper services

Figure 6.3. *(continued)*

If you have a question that is not addressed here or in the Guidelines for Journal Authors' Rights, please contact:

Permissions Department

University of Chicago Press, Journals Division

1427 East 60th Street, Chicago, IL 60637

Email: journalpermissions@press.uchicago.edu

GUIDELINES FOR JOURNAL AUTHORS' RIGHTS

Last updated August 2, 2021

All authors who publish an article in a journal published by The University of Chicago Press have certain rights to use their articles for research, teaching, and scholarly purposes. Your rights are governed by your publication agreement or license and by the provisions of these Guidelines, as in effect at the time of your proposed use of your article. These Guidelines address the questions we hear most often from authors about their rights to reuse their articles. If you have a question that is not addressed here, please contact:

Permissions Department

University of Chicago Press, Journals Division

1427 East 60th Street, Chicago, IL 60637

Email: journalpermissions@press.uchicago.edu

Key Concepts

Manuscript Version: What you are permitted to do with your manuscript or article depends in part on the version that you intend to use. The versions referred to in these guidelines are defined as follows:

Author's Original Manuscript (AOM): Any version of the manuscript, such as a working paper, before it is submitted to a journal for consideration for publication. The AOM is a **preacceptance** version.

Prior publication: We encourage you to consult the journal's editor before posting online a paper intended for submission to one of our journals. In some cases, such posting may constitute **prior publication** —for example, posting a working paper to a venue with a formal review and accreditation process. In addition, posting a paper intended for submission may compromise the confidentiality of the refereeing process if the journal uses an anonymous (blind) peer review system and delay or prevent a decision based on the paper's merits. You should disclose to the journal editor any prior publication or posting of your manuscript.

(continued)

Figure 6.3. *(continued)*

Sample Copyright Ownership Policies

Author's Submitted Manuscript (ASM): The version of the manuscript that is submitted to a journal for consideration for publication, prior to editorial (peer) review. The ASM is a **preacceptance** version.

> **Concurrent submission**: Submitting the same paper to more than one journal concurrently is a violation of the Press's ethical standards. Any such manuscript will be rejected. For more information, see the Press's Statement of Publication Ethics.

Author's Accepted Manuscript (AAM): The version of the manuscript that is accepted for publication in the journal, after editorial (peer) review and prior to copyediting. All authors must sign a publication agreement or license when the manuscript is accepted, indicating acceptance of the terms in the publication agreement or license and these Guidelines. The AAM is a **postacceptance** version.

Proofs: Some journals may provide you with typeset proofs of your article before it is published. Because proofs are under embargo and easily confused with the version of record (VoR—see below), proofs may not be posted, shared, or otherwise used except as directed by the editorial office or the Press.

Version of Record (VoR): The published article, regardless of format or medium of publication (e.g., print, PDF, HTML, MOBI, EPUB). Your rights to reuse the VoR depend in part on the format of the VoR that you wish to use and whether the VoR is accessible by subscription only or as open or free access. The VoR is a **postacceptance** version.

Citation, Abstract, Link (CAL): A citation (or reference)—the bibliographic information about the published article, including author(s), title, journal, volume and issue, date of publication, Digital Object Identifier (DOI), URL of the VoR, and the abstract. For journals without an abstract, an author-generated summary or the first page of the published PDF may be used.

Publication Date: The publication date of an article is the date on which the VoR is posted to the journal's website. Ahead-of-print articles (that is, VoR articles that are posted before release of the issue in which the article appears) are considered to be published. Some journals may post the AAM prior to release of the VoR, usually under the heading Just Accepted; these manuscripts are not considered to be published.

Open Access or Free Access: These terms both refer to free distribution of an article on the internet: making it available for free, with no payment required to read or access the article. We use the term free access when we make an article freely available, either permanently or temporarily, at the direction of the journal's editor, sponsor, or publisher. We use the term open access when we make an article freely and permanently available at the request of the author. Gold open access means

Figure 6.3. *(continued)*

making the VoR freely and permanently available on the journal's website starting at the time of publication, after payment of a fee (often called an Article Processing or Publication Charge, or APC). Green open access means making a version of the article, usually the AAM and less commonly the VoR, freely and permanently available on a third-party website, such as an institutional repository. There are no author fees for green open access, although certain conditions apply (see Deposit to a Repository or Preprint/Working Paper Service). Our default policy for green open access allows authors to comply with common institutional or funding agency open access mandates.

View more information about open or free access at the Press.

Creative Commons (or equivalent) License: A license that specifies how your article may be used by a third party. View information about the various Creative Commons (CC) licenses.

It is important to understand the distinction between copyright, CC licenses, and access, as these concepts are frequently confused. Copyright refers to ownership of a work (including the case of no ownership, or public domain). A CC license placed on a work tells other people how they may use the work. Access refers to the distribution of the work or the way others may gain access to it. Each of these concepts is independent of the others, even if in practice some combinations are more common than others. So, for example, the publication of an article as open access does not mean that the author is the copyright holder (although the author may be). Similarly, an article that is in the public domain, perhaps because the author is an employee of the United States federal government, does not have to be published as open or free access. The application of a CC license to an article does not mean the article is free of copyright, nor does the use of a CC license require that the article be published as open or free access. The CC license does not indicate the copyright status of the article and is not tied to copyright ownership or copyright transfer.

We apply a CC license to any article that is published as gold open access. If you request that the VoR of your article be published as gold open access and that request is approved, the article will normally be made available (after payment of the appropriate fee) under a Creative Commons Attribution-NonCommercial 4.0 International License (CC BY-NC 4.0). Under this license, any reuse of the VoR must credit the author and the journal. Commercial reuse requires permission from the Press.

If you wish to publish your article using a different license, you must notify the journal's editor at the time that it is accepted.

Institutional or Funder Mandate: You may be subject to a mandate or prior license from your institution or funder. Such directives may claim certain reuse rights to your work or require you to make some version of your paper available as open access, sometimes under a specific CC license. You will be asked to disclose any such mandates or licenses to the editorial office of the journal prior to signing the

Figure 6.3. *(continued)*

(continued)

Sample Copyright Ownership Policies   **69**

publication agreement or license for your manuscript. If the terms of your mandate conflict with the terms described in this policy—if, for example, you are expected to post some version of your paper in an open access repository with a postpublication embargo shorter than 12 months—you should first apply for any available waivers to the mandate.

Repositories and Preprint/Working Paper Services: Both repositories and preprint/working paper services are platforms used for the systematic archiving, retrieval, and delivery of a corpus of scholarly material. This is distinct from a personal, departmental, or social media web page or a third-party commercial article distribution platform such as Academia.edu or ResearchGate. A repository can be used as a site for the deposit of published works (AAM, VoR, CAL), whereas a preprint/working paper service offers a platform for authors or institutions to communicate works in progress (AOM, ASM). Some services may function as both a repository and a preprint or working paper service (such as arXiv or Humanities Commons). A service may be used to highlight a particular institution's output (such as Harvard University's DASH repository or The World Bank's Open Knowledge Repository) or it may be discipline-specific (such as BioArXiv or AgEcon). Repositories and preprint/working paper services may be operated by academic institutions, scholarly societies, government bodies, or businesses. Your right to deposit your article in any such service is determined by the version of your article that you post and whether the service is operated in a noncommercial manner. Noncommercial means the service does not financially benefit from commercial operations (e.g., by charging access fees, by charging fees for the distribution or aggregation of material, by selling advertising, or by selling user data).

Use for Teaching

You may use: AOM, ASM, AAM, VoR, CAL

Do not use: Proofs

You may use any version of your article (except proofs) for teaching purposes. There is no postpublication embargo on use of the VoR for this purpose. Allowable use includes:

- making copies for each student, either individually or as part of a printed course pack
- making the article available through print or electronic reserve or on a learning management platform

Conditions:

- Copies of the article must be used solely for classes you teach, unless you are using the AOM or any version of the article made available under a CC BY license.
- Classes must be academic and noncommercial in nature (for example, continuing education courses run for certification purposes would require additional permission), unless you are using the AOM or any version of the article made available under a CC BY license.

Figure 6.3. *(continued)*

- Access to all versions except AOM, open or free access VoR, CAL, or any version of the article made available under a CC BY license must be restricted to registered students.
- Copies must indicate the copyright holder (shown in the copyright notice at the foot of the article) and any applicable license and include a link to the VoR or the article DOI if available.
- If you included copyrighted material in your article with permission from the copyright holder, check the permission grant to see whether any restrictions apply to your reuse of the content.

Use in Presentations

You may use: AOM, ASM, AAM, VoR, CAL

Do not use: Proofs

You may use any version of your article (except proofs) in oral presentations or webinars. There is no postpublication embargo on use of the VoR for this purpose. Allowable use includes:

- making copies for members of the audience
- including excerpts in shareable presentation slides

Conditions:

- Access to all versions except AOM, open or free access VoR, CAL, or any version of the article made available under a CC BY license must be restricted to members of the audience.
- You must indicate the copyright holder (shown in the copyright notice at the foot of the article) and any applicable license and include a link to the VoR or the article DOI if available.
- If you included copyrighted material in your article with permission from the copyright holder, check the permission grant to see whether any restrictions apply to your reuse of the content

Send to Colleagues

You may use: AOM, ASM, AAM, VoR, CAL

Do not use: Proofs

You may provide single copies of any version of your article (except proofs) in either print or electronic form to a limited number of your colleagues for the purposes of scholarly discussion. There is no postpublication embargo on use of the VoR for this purpose.

Conditions:

- Copies may not be provided for compensation, except for any version of the article made available under a CC BY license.

(continued)

Figure 6.3. *(continued)*

- Copies may not be provided for the purposes of republication or preparing derivative work, except for any version of the article made available under a CC BY license.

- Copies may not be provided as part of the systematic provision of copyrighted material to a third party, nor to a third party that facilitates large-scale distribution of copyrighted material, except for any version of the article made available under a CC BY license.

- You must indicate the copyright holder and journal name (shown in the copyright notice at the foot of the article) and any applicable license and include a link to the VoR or the article DOI if available.

- If you included copyrighted material in your article with permission from the copyright holder, check the permission grant to see whether any restrictions apply to your reuse of the content.

- Further restrictions apply to use of your article on social media sites such as Academia.edu, ResearchGate, LinkedIn, and Facebook. See Post on Social Media Platforms for more information.

Share with News Media

You may use: AOM, ASM, AAM, VoR, CAL

Do not use: Proofs

We encourage you to share the published results of your research with the news media. To help you get started, you may wish to view our authors resources page. Our marketing department can help you or your institution's news office identify news sources, blogs, and other relevant outlets that may be interested in your research.

Authors and their institutions should exercise caution, however, when discussing unpublished work with the news media. You should make clear that the work is preliminary and that the conclusions may change after peer review. You should not solicit media coverage of prepublication manuscripts. Discussion of unpublished research may compromise the confidentiality of the refereeing process if the journal uses an anonymous (blind) peer review system and delay or prevent a decision based on the paper's merits

Some journals may require you to keep the acceptance of your manuscript confidential prior to publication. A prepublication media embargo may also be imposed. You or your institution's news office should consult the journal's editorial office before releasing any information about a manuscript accepted for publication but not yet published.

Figure 6.3. *(continued)*

Conditions:

- Full text of postacceptance versions (AAM, VoR) cannot be shared with news media prior to publication.
- AAM, VoR: cannot be posted on news sites, blogs, or other media outlets without permission of the Press, except for any version available under a CC BY license.
- You should include a link to the VoR on the journal's website or the article DOI in your communication with the news media. News reports should not link to prepublication versions of your work or any version available on a site other than the journal's website.

Republish or Adapt Excerpts or Entire Article

You have the nonexclusive right to republish your article, in whole or in part, in a form identical to the VoR or any previous version or as a new adaptation or derivative, in any subsequent book, article, or other scholarly work of which you are an author or an editor, including your dissertation, provided that appropriate credit is given to the journal as follows:

- Republication of the VoR without modifications: indicate the copyright holder (shown in the copyright notice at the foot of the article) and any applicable license and include a link to the VoR or the article DOI if available.
- If the article has not yet been published, include a statement specifying the article's status, date, and journal name. For example: "Submitted (or Accepted) for publication to (by) Journal Name on MM/DD/YYYY." Include the article DOI if available.
- Republication of an adaptation or derivative version: include a statement identifying the new work as an adaptation or derivative and crediting the journal as the first instance of publication. Include the copyright holder (shown in the copyright notice at the foot of the article) and any applicable license and include a link to the VoR or the article DOI if available.

Conditions:

- Some journals have an embargo period after publication of the VoR before the article can appear in another publication. Consult the editorial office.
- You may republish the VoR or a version substantially the same as it in an open access publication only with permission from the Press and with a CC BY-NC 4.0 license or equivalent, unless the VoR was published under a CC BY license.
- The author's right of republication does not apply to the author's institution or employer, including when the paper is a work made for hire, unless the VoR was published under a CC BY license. If your institution or funder claims republication rights through a mandate or prior license, and you have requested but not been granted a waiver to that policy, then the institution or funder's claim is limited to the AOM or ASM except with permission of the Press.
- If you included copyrighted material in your article with permission from the copyright holder, check the permission grant to see whether any restrictions apply to your reuse of the content. Further permission is often required for republication of such content.

Figure 6.3. *(continued)*

(continued)

Deposit to a Repository or Preprint/Working Paper Service

You may use: AAM, VoR, CAL (repository); AOM, ASM (preprint/working paper service)

Do not use: Proofs

You may deposit pre- and postacceptance versions of your article to a repository or preprint/working paper service, provided you observe the conditions set out below. Your right to deposit your article in any such service is determined by the version of your article that you post and whether the service is operated in a noncommercial manner.

Third-party article sharing platforms such as Academia.edu and ResearchGate do not qualify as repositories or preprint/working paper services. For conditions on posting to such sites, see Post on Social Media Platforms.

Conditions on posting preacceptance versions (AOM, ASM):

- We urge you to use caution before posting preacceptance versions of your paper to a preprint or working paper service. Posting a paper intended for submission (AOM) may compromise the confidentiality of the refereeing process if the journal uses an anonymous (blind) peer review system and delay or prevent a decision based on the paper's merits.
- Posting may constitute prior publication, particularly if the posted version of your paper is assigned a DOI; undergoes editorial or peer review; or is released under the service's imprimatur (such as a numbered Working Paper series).
- If the manuscript has been submitted to a journal, you must include a statement specifying the paper's status, date, and journal name. For example: "Submitted for publication to Journal Name on MM/DD/YYYY." The statement should be updated with any change in your paper's publication status, unless the journal requires you to keep the acceptance of your manuscript confidential.
- The working paper should be made available only under the CC BY-NC 4.0 license or equivalent. If an alternate license was used and the working paper cannot be removed from the platform once the VoR is published, you should change the license of the working paper to CC BY-NC 4.0 or equivalent, if possible.
- You should remove the working paper from the service after your article is published, if possible. If the service acts as a repository for postacceptance works as well as a preprint service, you may replace the working paper with a postacceptance version (AAM, VoR, CAL), provided you observe the conditions below.
- If you included copyrighted material in your article with permission from the copyright holder, check the permission grant to see whether any restrictions apply to your posting of the content. Further permission may be required, particularly if the manuscript is made available as open access.

Figure 6.3. *(continued)*

Conditions on posting postacceptance versions (AAM, VoR, CAL):

- Postacceptance versions may be posted to institutional or discipline-specific repositories or services that are operated in a noncommercial manner, meaning the service does not financially benefit from commercial operations (e.g., by charging access fees, by charging fees for the distribution or aggregation of material, by selling advertising, or by selling user data). Most repositories run by academic institutions or government agencies (such as PubMed Central) are acceptable, but many services offered by commercial enterprises (such as SSRN) are not.
- AAM or subscription or free access VoR: may be placed in the repository upon publication of the VoR with a 12-month postpublication embargo on public availability.
- Open access VoR or CAL: may be placed in the repository upon publication of the VoR with no embargo on public availability.
- You must apply for any available waivers from your funding body or institution if they <u>require</u> a prepublication deposit and/or a postpublication embargo of less than 12 months. If a waiver is not granted, you may deposit your article according to the terms of the mandate, but in that case, <u>only</u> the AAM or open access VoR may be deposited.
- Your article should be made available only under a CC BY-NC 4.0 license or equivalent, except in the following cases:
  - The VoR is published under a different license, in which case you should use that license.
  - Your funding body or institution requires an alternate license such as a CC BY license <u>and</u> you have applied for (if possible) but been denied permission to use a CC BY-NC license. If you make your article available under any license other than a CC BY-NC license, <u>only</u> the AAM may be posted.
- You must indicate the copyright holder and journal name (usually shown in the copyright notice at the foot of the article) and any applicable license and include a link to the VoR or the article DOI if available.
- If you included copyrighted material in your article with permission from the copyright holder, check the permission grant to see whether any restrictions apply to your posting of the content. Further permission may be required, particularly if the manuscript in the repository is made available as open access.

Post on Personal or Departmental Web Page

You may use: AOM, ASM, AAM, VoR, CAL

Do not use: Proofs

You may post any version of your article (except proofs) on your personal or departmental web page, but we strongly encourage you to post only the CAL and link to the VoR. Strong online usage statistics, which are very important for tracking readership of your paper, play a vital role in identifying where your work may be making its strongest impact—but the ability to gain such data is lost with an easily pirated PDF.

(continued)

Figure 6.3. (continued)

Sample Copyright Ownership Policies

Conditions:

- Personal web pages offered through a social media or article-sharing platform do not qualify, except for the AOM, ASM, CAL, or any version of the article made available under a CC BY license. See Post on Social Media Platforms for more information.
- Preacceptance versions (AOM, ASM) may be posted at any time. If you post the ASM, include a statement specifying the paper's status, date, and journal name. For example: "Submitted for publication to Journal Name on MM/DD/YYYY."
- AAM: may be posted only upon publication of the VoR. Include a statement specifying the paper's status, date, and journal name. For example: "Accepted for publication by Journal Name on MM/DD/YYYY." Include the copyright notice at the foot of the article and a link to the VoR on the journal website or the article DOI.
- VoR: may be posted only after a postpublication embargo period of 12 months unless the VoR is published as open access or with a CC BY license. Include a link to the VoR on the journal website or the article DOI.
- If you included copyrighted material in your article with permission from the copyright holder, check the permission grant to see whether any restrictions apply to your posting of the content. Further permission may be required, particularly if the manuscript is made available as open access on your personal or departmental web page.
- We encourage you to consult the journal's editor before posting the AOM on your personal or departmental web page. Posting a paper intended for submission may compromise the confidentiality of the refereeing process if the journal uses an anonymous (blind) peer review system and delay or prevent a decision based on the paper's merits.

Post on Social Media Platforms

You may use: AOM, ASM, CAL

Do not use: Proofs, AAM, VoR, except for any version made available under a CC-BY license

You may post only the AOM, ASM, CAL, or any version of the article made available under a CC BY license on social media or article-sharing platforms including, but not limited to, Facebook, Twitter, LinkedIn, Academia.edu, and ResearchGate.

Conditions:

- You may not post the full text of any postacceptance version of your article (AAM, VoR) on social media or article-sharing platforms, except for any version made available under a CC BY license.
- We encourage you to consult the journal's editor before posting the AOM to such platforms, as posting a paper intended for submission may compromise the confidentiality of the refereeing process if the journal uses an anonymous (blind) peer review system and delay or prevent a decision based on the paper's merits.

Figure 6.3. *(continued)*

NOTE

1. California Institute of the Arts. "Policy on Ownership of Copyright and Sale of Objects of Art Created by Members of the Institute." Accessed March 31, 2023, https://policies.calarts.edu/all-policies/institute-affairs-policy-on-ownership-copyright-and-sale-of-objects-of-art-created-by-members-of-the-institute.

7

Sample Authorship Policies

This chapter offers a look at how academic institutions, journals, and publishers have addressed equity, diversity, and inclusion within authorship policies. The sample policies included in this chapter provide useful approaches to accurately defining authorship and encouraging research groups to be more equitable and inclusive of all types of authors. In addition, the institutional policies included here all have sections on authorship disputes, which signals that decision-making on authorship within research groups calls for stronger and clearer practices. In my research on lab-based policies, only a handful could be located on the web, limiting this chapter primarily to institutional, journal, and publisher policies.

As we have seen in previous chapters, approaches to authorship within labs and research groups stand as the fundamental site requiring clear policies and practices. Since most lab managers have expertise in a discipline or sub-discipline but may not have expertise in how copyright ownership and joint authorship work, this becomes an important aspect of establishing well-defined policies. In addition, most institutions place nearly all of the publication decision-making authority on the principal investigator or lab manager. Lack of familiarity with copyright ownership along with sole decision-making authority can set the stage for potentially confusing and inequitable authorship experiences.

In the few examples from labs and research groups posted publicly on the web, many of them did not accurately define authorship. This could lead to the potential of ghost authorship (i.e., leaving off legitimate authors) or gifting authorship (i.e., listing someone who has not fully contributed to a work of authorship). In one example, a lab policy indicated that authorship was conferred when one made significant contribution to at least two of the five areas identified by the lab manager: conception, design, execution, analysis, and reporting. But in this model, if one had only contributed to reporting, that alone would be sufficient for co-authorship, leaving the lab with the potential of ghosting a legitimate author, resulting in inaccurate and unfair treatment. In another example, a lab introduced the concept of doing more than was expected of a student enrolled at the lab's institution as a condition of authorship, which equates authorship with rewards and establishes conditions for inequities within a research group.

In another lab policy, the lab conveyed their authorship practice simply as a weighted model with writing weighted the most heavily and data analysis and gathering weighted the least. Yes, writing represents a copyrightable contribution to a work of authorship and because of that should be explicitly stated as a given of how copyright and joint authorship operate. If you write a work, that makes you an author. But what if you do not contribute by writing, but only by conceptualizing the research inquiry or gathering and analyzing data? That still represents an intellectual contribution and can become an issue of equity and inclusion within authorship. Spelling out more clearly what is meant by contributing by means of idea generation or gathering data and analyzing it would make such a policy much stronger. Better yet, an even clearer policy would simply indicate that writing a portion of the shared work of authorship remains a requirement of the lab or research group. In other words, no one gets out of writing when it comes to creating scholarly works of authorship. Keeping a lab policy clear and simple is imperative, but not so simple that terms go undefined or basic elements such as shared copyright ownership go unmentioned. Table 7.1 provides tips on how to avoid ghosting and gifting authorship and can be used to establish written policies and practices within a research group setting.

Table 7.1. How to Avoid Ghosting and Gifting Authorship

Tips for Creating Inclusive and Equitable Authorship Practices
Know who generated the research idea or line of inquiry.
Be aware of who gathered data and/or analyzed it for the project.
Determine writing assignments based on data-gathering role.
Keep track of who wrote each section of the work.
Include as co-authors those who have written sections of the report; also consider who developed the research idea.
Identify those who contributed data or analysis but did not write; include them in the acknowledgments section.
Establish equitable author order based on data-gathering role + writing assignment.

INSTITUTIONAL AUTHORSHIP POLICIES

Authorship policies within an academic institution will focus on the expectations for research managers who oversee collaborations involving students and faculty. They typically provide some direction on what might constitute authorship as well as equity within authorship with the expectation that authors-as-conveners will develop more tailored definitions and communicate those definitions with those involved in the project.

UNIVERSITY OF TOLEDO—GUIDELINES ON AUTHORSHIP

The University of Toledo's policy serves as an excellent example of encouraging both equity and accuracy within authorship practices. It does so by establishing a policy goal, setting it as an institutional priority, and including the term "equitable" when discussing the role of the project lead. That role, as we will see throughout the rest of the policy examples in this chapter, is the role of author-as-convener and it is that person who needs to have a deep understanding of equity within the scholarly communication process.

Name of Policy: Guidelines on authorship	
Policy Number: 3364-71-29	**UT** THE UNIVERSITY OF **TOLEDO** 1872
Approving Officer: President	
Responsible Agent: Vice Provost for Graduate Affairs and Dean, College of Graduate Studies; Provost and Executive Vice President for Academic Affairs	**Effective date**: June 27, 2022 **Original effective date:** June 27, 2022
Scope: All University of Toledo campuses	

X	New policy proposal		Minor/technical revision of existing policy
	Major revision of existing policy		Reaffirmation of existing policy

    (A)   Policy statement

            Our institution's academic mission emphasizes the importance of the creation and dissemination of new knowledge through publications, creative work, intellectual property, and other discipline-specific scholarly activities. Assigning credit and appropriate recognition for scholarly work through authorship is a priority of the University of Toledo.

    (B)   Purpose of policy

            To establish general guidelines for authorship in research and scholarly work and to outline a process for authorship disputes at the University of Toledo.

(continued)

Figure 7.1. University of Toledo's Guidelines on Authorship

(C)   Scope

These authorship guidelines are applicable to any scholarly or research activity (e.g., publications, creative expressions, presentations or the disciplinary equivalent) carried out by faculty, staff, and students at the University of Toledo. The term scholarly activity also includes research activities.

(D)   Publication & Authorship

The University of Toledo strongly recommends that discussions of authorship occur at the initiation of new projects and when roles or responsibilities change during the project. The project lead, principal investigator, corresponding author, or equivalent should ensure that procedures for resolving detailed concerns, such as the timing of presentations or publications, order of authorship, and privilege of presenting results at meetings, be discussed with research team members to the extent feasible at the beginning and throughout the scholarly activities as needed and as part of on-boarding new members to the research group or project.

The project lead or principal investigator has the responsibility to ensure that all scholarly work is accurately reported and that apportioning of credit for the work accomplished is equitable and in conformance with best practices, recognizing the existence discipline-specific conventions regarding authorship and attribution. Explicitly stating the role and contribution of each author will enhance the transparency and credibility of the work as well as accurately assign credit for purposes of individual and collective academic advancement.

Authorship should be based on the following general criteria: (i) substantial intellectual contribution to conception, design, or execution of the work (including data analysis); (ii) drafting or revising the work for important content; and (iii) final approval of the version to be published. Each co-author should have the ability to identify their contribution to the scholarly work, to identify the significance of the contributions of each author, and to accept responsibility for its integrity and credibility. Individuals who do not meet all these criteria may be acknowledged as contributors to the work. The primary or corresponding author generally has the greatest understanding of the project, completed most of the work, and takes responsibility for the integrity of the work as a whole. In addition, primary authors are encouraged to keep a record of how decisions about authorship order and inclusion were made.

1. Acquisition of financial sponsorship, donation of gift funding, or receipt of materials does not constitute criteria for authorship. Individuals who do not meet the recommended requirements for authorship, but have provided a valuable contribution to the work, should be acknowledged for their contributing role as appropriate to the publication.
2. Guest, gift and ghost authorship are inconsistent with the definition of authorship. Guest or gift authorship (i.e., honorary, courtesy or prestige authorship) is granting authorship to an individual who does not meet the definition of author. Guest authorship is often given out of appreciation or respect for the individual, in the belief that the expert standing of the co-author will increase the likelihood of publication, credibility, or status of the work, or to assist junior colleagues, students, or mentees to further their careers.
3. Ghost authorship is the opposite of honorary or gift authorship when an individual is not named an author or properly acknowledged but makes significant contributions to the work. A role in writing or editing a manuscript, poster, or presentation without a contribution to the intellectual endeavor that constitutes the work may not arise to inclusion as an author under these guidelines. Individuals who meet the criteria of authorship should be listed as an author or otherwise have their contribution properly acknowledged in the publication. Egregious occurrences of ghost authorship may constitute research misconduct. The definition of an author for copyright purposes may differ from scholarly norms and should be considered separately.
4. The primary or corresponding author or equivalent must ensure that all co-authors on publications or presentations have been informed of their inclusion as authors and that all authors have reviewed materials prior to publication and presentation. Failure to do so could constitute research misconduct. The primary or corresponding author or equivalent should make efforts to notify other individuals who are acknowledged in the publication or presentation as to the nature and extent of their acknowledgement.

(E)   Authorship Disputes

Authorship disputes are considered academic matters at the University of Toledo. When co-authors cannot address disagreements through collegial resolution, they should seek guidance from a third party (e.g., department chair, senior colleague) acceptable to all parties. If no resolution can be reached at the local level, the matter should be forwarded to the dean(s) of the appropriate colleges for external guidance. Students are encouraged to seek advice from the Office of Student Advocacy and Support. If a

Figure 7.1. *(continued)*

resolution is reached, the agreement must be documented, signed by all parties, and a copy should be sent to the Office of the Provost. If agreement cannot be reached to the satisfaction of all parties, the matter will be referred to Provost's Office.

Within twenty-five (25) working days, the Provost or the Provost's designee will establish a committee comprised of at least three faculty members. If one of the parties is without faculty rank (e.g., student, postdoctoral researcher, or research staff), the committee shall also include at least two representative individuals. Most of the committee shall be comprised of faculty engaged in scholarship, at least one of whom is outside the discipline of the parties in the dispute. Committee members may include non-tenure-track faculty, students, or administrators. The committee will seek written statements from all who claim to be co-authors in the dispute. All who claim to be co-authors must be notified at last known contact information by the University and given the opportunity to present their case in writing within 10 business days of letters being sent from the Committee..

After the committee meets to review the submitted materials, a written report including a majority decision will becommunicated to the Provost within 15 working days. The Provost will provide a written summary of the committee decision to the partiesinvolved within fifteen (15) working days of receiving the final decision. The Provost's decision will be final.

Authorship disputes that involve research misconduct as defined in the University Policy on integrity in research and procedures for investigating allegations of misconduct (#3364-70-21) must be referred to and addressed by the Universityof Toledo Research Integrity Officer (RIO). Authorship disputes that do not meet the definition of research misconduct but still demonstrate that there was inappropriate conduct as it related to authorship should refer to the University Policy on Standards of Conduct (#3364-25-01).

(F)   Disclosures & Affiliations

Authors should acknowledge the sources of support for all activities leading to and facilitating preparation of the presentation, publication or manuscript, including, but not limited to grant, contract, gift support; salary support, if other than institutional funds; and technical or other support if substantive and meaningful to the completion of the project. Authors should fully disclose related financial and other interests and outside activities in publications and comply with the disclosure requirements of the University's Conflict of Interest Committee as appropriate. University policy 3364-70-01, Financial Conflict of Interest provides further guidance.

University faculty, staff and other employees with 50% employment or greater must list their affiliation with the University of Toledo, with the name of the institution written out in full, as their primary affiliation in their by-line on any research or scholarly output conducted or performed during their employment at the University. Students, full or part-time, must list their affiliation with the University of Toledo, with the name of the institution written out in full, as their primary affiliation in their by-line on any research or scholarly output conducted or performed through the University. In these cases, if multiple affiliations exist, the University of Toledo must be listed first. This requirement also applies to research and scholarly activity conducted primarily at the University and published after faculty, staff or students have left the institution unless the publication, presentation, or sponsor requires otherwise.

Approved by:	Policies Superseded by This Policy:
/s/ Gregory Postel, MD President	*None* **Initial effective date**: June 27, 2022 **Review/revision date**: NA
June 27, 2022 Date	**Next review date**: June 27, 2025
Review/Revision Completed by: Vice Provost for Graduate Affairs and Dean, College of Graduate Studies; Provost and Executive Vice President for Academic Affairs; Senior Leadership Team	

Figure 7.1. *(continued)*

UNIVERSITY OF UTAH—DETERMINING AUTHORSHIP IN SCHOLARLY OR SCIENTIFIC PUBLICATIONS

The University of Utah's policy provides another example of the importance of referencing fairness and equity within authorship practices. It highlights the role of the research manager in ensuring equitable practices, but also brings in the academic unit or department in setting authorship policies at that level so that the individual manager has support from other researchers and from the institution.

Policy 7-020: Determining Authorship in Scholarly or Scientific Publications.

Revision 0. Effective date: April 13, 2021

View PDF

I. Purpose and Scope

    A. Purpose.

An important component of ensuring the integrity of the research and scholarly enterprise is determining authorship, because determination of authorship provides evidence of assigning responsibility and giving credit for intellectual work. Authorship credit should be given to those who contribute to and participate in substantive ways to scholarly and scientific work, and the relative credit given should honestly and accurately reflect actual contributions. Fair and equitable determination of authorship is important to the reputation, academic promotion, and funding support of the individuals involved, and to the strength and reputation of the authors' respective institutions.

Authorship confers credit for contributions and has important academic, social, and financial implications. Authorship also implies responsibility and accountability for published work. The University recognizes that authorship is important for faculty academic careers and the lack of clear guidance for determining authorship may lead to unnecessary conflicts among contributors. Disagreements sometimes arise regarding who should ultimately be named as an author of or contributor to intellectual work and the relative order in which individuals should be listed. Some of these disputes are a result of failure of early communication and expectation-setting.

This Policy is meant to provide both procedures and a set of standards that are shared by the University's academic community as a whole, to help facilitate open communication through adherence to common principles. These principles apply to all intellectual products, whether published or prepared for internal use or for broad dissemination.

Designing an ethical and transparent approach to determining authorship for publication of research results is primarily the responsibility of the principal investigator(s). This Policy and its associated Regulations are intended to outline the ethical responsibilities of the investigator(s), and describe some of the University of Utah resources available to support implementation of the principles outlined herein.

    B. Scope.

This Policy applies to all faculty members, students, postdoctoral fellows and other non-faculty academic-employees (see Policy 6-309), and staff employees of the University of Utah.

Figure 7.2. University of Utah's Policy on Determining Authorship in Scholarly or Scientific Publications

This Policy regarding authorship is not intended to directly govern issues of the ownership of data and materials produced in the course of research activities, which issues are instead governed by other University Regulations. (See Policy 7-002 for patents and inventions and Policy 7-003 for Copyright ownership).

This Policy is intended to be implemented through associated Regulations, and Guidance documents developed by the relevant administrative officers (primarily the Vice President for Research). The Policy will be reviewed every five years by the Academic Senate for revisions and changes as needed for determining authorship.

Because the University recognizes that authorship practices may be very different for different disciplines and attempting to apply specific requirements regarding determination of authorship over multiple disciplines would not be the appropriate approach, this Policy sets forth certain generally applicable principles, and then requires the various academic units of the University to develop internal regulations appropriate for the particular disciplines, in the form of Supplemental Rules supplementing this Policy. In the event a particular academic unit does not develop internal regulations appropriate for its discipline, the principles and rules set forth herein, and in the accompanying Guideline(s) will govern.

II. Definitions

The following definitions apply for the limited purposes of this policy and any associated regulations.

A. Authorship confers intellectual credit, responsibility, and accountability for published work.

III. Policy

A. Criteria for Determining Authorship.

  1. Supplemental Rules of internal policies developed by departments or other academic units.

      a. Each academic department or other academic unit (as described in Policy 6-001) whose members regularly participate in research/creative activity shall adopt a written internal policy to govern determinations of authorship for the members of the faculty, non-faculty academic personnel, staff, and students of that academic unit, which must be consistent with this Policy 7-020 and other University Regulations, and should be consistent with the established practices of the academic discipline(s). It is recommended that the principles and criteria for determining authorship follow those of the leading academic societies and journals relevant to the unit's academic discipline(s).

      b. The internal policy of each unit (and any subsequent revision) should be approved by the voting faculty members of the academic unit. An internal policy may be approved by the voting faculty of each academic department and each other unit within an entire college. If so approved, it will function as a college-wide internal policy.

      c. Once so approved by the relevant voting faculty, the internal policy will constitute a Supplemental Rule of the academic unit for implementation of this Policy 7-020 (see Policy 1-001 describing such supplemental rules). A copy of the current Supplemental Rule of each unit shall be provided to the unit administrator and college dean (or equivalent positions), office for Faculty Affairs, and the office of the Vice President for Research, and shall be included with the documentation provided by the unit for each seven-year review (commonly known as a Graduate Council Review). The consistency of practices under that Supplemental Rule shall be considered in such seven- year reviews of the academic unit. The unit's administrators should make reasonable efforts to ensure that faculty members, and other members of the unit regularly participating in research/creative activities are aware of the unit's internal policy and practices.

  2. University-wide Recommended Criteria. The University recommends that determinations of authorship be based on the following four criteria, defined by the International Committee for Medical Journal Editors (ICMJE):

      a. Substantial contributions to the conception or design of the work; or the acquisition, analysis, or interpretation of data for the work;

      b. Drafting the work or revising it critically for important intellectual content;

      c. Final approval of the version to be published; and

      d. Agreement to be accountable for all aspects of the work in ensuring that questions related to the accuracy or integrity of any part of the work are appropriately investigated and resolved.

  3. Resources for Additional Criteria. The Office of the Vice President for Research may advise members of the University community regarding other available resources for developing clear criteria. Currently those resources include the following (and this list may be updated as an editorial correction of this Policy at the direction of the Vice President for Research).

      a. The International Committee for Medical Journal Editors (ICMJE) provides comprehensive instruction on authorship which may be accessed on its website (at www.icmje.org).

      b. The Consortia Advancing Standards in research Administration Information (CASRAI) highlights activities that individuals must complete to be considered a contributor to intellectual work (available at https://casrai.org/credit/).

      c. The American Psychological Association (APA) recommends developing a contract for authorship, and provides a model form (available at: http://www.apa.org/science/leadership/students/authorship- agreement.pdf).

(continued)

Figure 7.2. *(continued)*

B. Policy Implementation.

   1. Successful implementation of this Policy and associated Regulations relies on a commitment to collegiality and open, frank, consistent communication and expectation-setting throughout the research and scholarly process. Integral to implementation of these Regulations are the following:

      a. Research groups should discuss authorship credit/criteria, presentation of joint work, and future directions of the research as early as practical, and frequently, during the course of their work. These discussions should involve explicit review of expectations of continued collaboration if a contributor who would normally be considered an author leaves the project or leaves the institution during the conduct of the work. The principal investigator or scholarly leader should initiate these discussions; however, any collaborator may raise questions or seek clarity throughout the course of the collaboration. Each laboratory or research group may consider having a written guiding document in place, consistent with this Policy and any relevant Supplemental Rule of an academic unit, and with guidance of the Vice President for Research.

      b. Collaborators are expected to adhere to good laboratory, archival and scholarly practices, including maintaining a complete laboratory notebook, research notes and annotating electronic files, as these practices will aide in identifying and clarifying individuals' contributions to a project.

      c. Disposition of collaborative data and research materials should be mutually agreed upon among collaborators as early as practical and in accordance with any data-sharing and retention requirements in the academic unit.

      d. Laboratory groups, academic departments, and other academic units or programs supporting research/creative activity at the University should include in any procedure manuals a copy of relevant Regulations, including this Policy 7-020 and any associated Guidelines, the applicable internal policies (Supplemental Rules) of relevant academic units, and if applicable a description of the group's own customary ways of deciding who should be an author and the order in which authors are listed. Those materials should be included in orientation of new members.

      e. Discussion of the principles of authorship as described in this Policy 7- 020 and associated Regulations, and other relevant University and academic unit policies should be integrated into any course regarding responsible conduct of research that is taught at the University.

C. Authorship Disputes and Resolution.

   1. Conflicts related to authorship may arise at any time during the research or scholarly process, resulting from differing perceptions of one's contributions and resulting attribution of credit. The University seeks to have dispute resolution procedures which lead to timely effective resolutions, facilitate excellence in research/creative activity, support collegial respectful relationships among participants, and in other respects serve the bests interests of the University. The University encourages parties to attempt the resolution of the dispute by working with the Office for Faculty in the office of the Senior Vice President for Academic Affairs, Office of Academic Affairs and Faculty Development in office of the Senior Vice President for Health Sciences, or the Graduate School to mediate between the parties. If such agreement cannot be reached the case will be referred to the Office of the Vice President of Research, that will have the primary administrative role in developing Rules, Procedures, or Guidance documents for dispute resolution methods to serve those ends, consistent with this Policy. If any party consider that his/her authorship rights have not been asserted by the decision of the VPR, by either not including the party as an author or by diluting his/her contribution to the work by the addition of authors to the work, the affected party can claim that his/her faculty rights have been affected by the VPR decision. The party will be able to seek further review of the case by the Senate Consolidated Hearing Committee (SCHC) under section III.B.3 (Complaint alleging violation of Faculty Code) of Policy 6-011. In the appeal the affected party should clearly indicate how the provision of the Faculty Code (Policy 6-316) section 4.C, 3-6 would apply to the case. The SCHC will make a final recommendation to the office of the President who will enforce recommendations. (Note that if a dispute involves an allegation of fabrication or falsification of data or plagiarism the dispute is subject to—Policy 7-001 Policy for Research Misconduct.)

      Sections IV- VII are for user information and are not subject to the approval of the Academic Senate or the Board of Trustees. The Institutional Policy Committee, the Policy Owner, or the Policy Officer may update these sections at any time.

IV. Policies/ Rules, Procedures, Guidelines, Forms and other Related Resources

   A. Policies/ Rules. [*reserved*]

   B. Procedures, Guidelines, and Forms.

      1. Guideline G7-020A: Determining Authorship in Scholarly or Scientific Publications including Resolution of Disputes Regarding Authorship

   C. Other Related Resources. [*reserved*]

Figure 7.2. *(continued)*

Figure 7.2. *(continued)*

UNIVERSITY OF TEXAS AT AUSTIN—AUTHORSHIP OF SCHOLARLY AND SCIENTIFIC PUBLICATIONS

The University of Texas at Austin's policy also mentions fairness but places more focus on accuracy. This is an additional and distinct example and approach to authorship policy practices. Accuracy is indeed an essential aspect of authorship and the policy provides additional direction for research managers to establish early communications with students and trainees on authorship expectations. This policy works in conjunction with the University of Texas System policy on copyright ownership detailed in chapter 6.

The University of Texas at Austin
University Policy Office
University Compliance Services

Handbook of Operating Procedures 7-1070
Authorship of Scholarly and Scientific Publications

Effective October 27, 2022
Executive Sponsor: Vice President for Research
Policy Owner: Director, Office of Research Support and Compliance

I. Policy Statement
Authorship is the primary means for assigning responsibility and credit for intellectual contributions to scholarly work. Public trust in research relies on the integrity of the research, including honesty and transparency in the dissemination of research results. Authorship attribution must be based on substantial, intellectual contribution to the work, and individuals accepting authorship credit must be willing to assume responsibility for the validity of research output. Appropriate authorship attribution and accurate disclosure of author affiliations are essential for enabling the scholarly community and the general public to identify those responsible for the disseminated work. All scholarly or scientific publications involving faculty, staff, students, and trainees arising from academic activities performed within the scope of institutional responsibilities at The University of Texas at Austin (University) must include appropriate authorship credit for individuals involved in the work and accurate disclosure of affiliation(s) for individuals identified as authors.

(continued)

Figure 7.3. University of Texas, Austin Authorship of Scholarly and Scientific Publications

II. Reason for Policy

To provide the institutional framework for rules and procedures for appropriate authorship attribution and reporting of institutional affiliation in the dissemination of scholarly and intellectual work.

III. Scope & Audience

This policy applies to all University faculty, staff, students, and trainees.

IV. Definitions (specific to this policy)

Institutional Responsibilities:
Any of the professional activities of a member of the University community, such as research, teaching, and service including membership on university committees and panels, as well as outward facing activities such as consulting, lecturing, and other pursuits related to the application of professional expertise.

Publication:
Includes articles, manuscripts and abstracts submitted for dissemination by a vehicle the discipline regards as a site for scholarly discourse; such as journals, websites, books, and others, as well as presentations at professional meetings and other venues.

V. Website (for policy)

https://secure2.compliancebridge.com/utexas/public/getdoc.php?file=7-1070

VI. Contacts

CONTACT	DETAILS	WEB
Office of Research Support and Compliance	Phone: 512-471-8871	Website: https://research.utexas.edu/ors

VII. Responsibilities & Procedures

A. Authorship Affiliation

Each author will report an affiliation when publishing or otherwise disseminating the results of research and scholarly activities. Ensuring accurate reporting of affiliations assigns credit to the institution(s) that contributed significantly or substantially to the work, whether through salary support, through the provision of resources, or by providing the appropriate intellectual environment. Faculty, staff, and students at The University of Texas at Austin should identify UT Austin as their primary affiliated institution with few exceptions as identified below.

Affiliations to other institutions should only be reported if the secondary institution made a substantive contribution to the specific publication, even if a formal relationship to that institution exists in other contexts. In situations where reporting multiple affiliations is appropriate, the primary affiliation should always be the institution where the majority of the work was completed or the institution that provided the greatest resource support, such as salary, research facilities, equipment and personnel. Guidelines for accurately reporting affiliations include:

- When considering dual affiliations, the primary affiliation should be identified as the institution paying more than ½ of an individual's salary over a 12-month period, including salary paid from sponsored research awards.
- University faculty and research scientists may not enter into contractual agreements with external entities that require identifying any entity other than UT Austin as the primary affiliation or that abridge publication and research rights as noted in Regents' *Rules and Regulations*, Rule 90101 - Intellectual Property. Exceptions to this rule can be made by the Office of Research Support and Compliance after approval from the department chair/unit director.
- Work substantively completed before joining UT Austin should identify the former institution as the primary affiliation and UT Austin as the secondary affiliation.
- Faculty conducting research while on a Faculty Research Assignment should identify UT Austin as the primary affiliation. A secondary affiliation may be noted if the research reported was partially supported by another institution.
- UT Austin faculty, students, and staff with guest, visiting, or adjunct positions at other institutions should identify UT Austin as their primary affiliation and identify the part-time institution as a secondary affiliation if that organization provided substantive support for the work or if much of the work was conducted at the other institution. In rare cases, the part-time institution may be the primary affiliation when a clear majority of the published work by the UT Austin employee was conducted at the part-time institution during a period where the employee was not paid by UT Austin. In these cases, explicit written approval from the department chair/unit director and the Office of Research Support and Compliance should be obtained.
- Doctoral students registered at or expecting to receive their degree from UT Austin should identify UT Austin as their primary affiliation.
- In all cases of dual affiliations, the non-University affiliation must be disclosed to the University according to HOP 5-2011 - Conflict of Interest, Conflict of Commitment, and Outside Activities, and HOP 7-1210 - Promoting Objectivity in Research by Managing, Reducing or Eliminating Financial Conflicts of Interest.

B. Authorship Credit

Authorship is the primary means by which the creation of scholarship and research is recognized in academia. Thus, it is imperative that authorship credit and order of authorship be assigned fairly and appropriately within best practice standards of the discipline. In general, authorship is granted to those individuals who have made a significant intellectual contribution and are willing to assume responsibility for the validity of the work. Authorship expectations, practices, and criteria should be discussed (and when possible, documented) among research teams and collaborators, including with students and trainees, early in the research process and throughout the conduct of the research as roles and responsibilities shift.

Individuals who make a significant contribution that does not rise to the level of authorship should be publicly acknowledged with their permission in advance of publication.

Further guidance on responsible authorship and authorship criteria is referenced in Section X. Related Information below.

C. Transparency and Disclosure

Transparency in disclosing significant financial relationships and other related outside affiliations is essential for maintaining trust in research output. Authors must disclose any interests that could be perceived as having an impact on the objectivity of the research as required by HOP 7-1210. All University personnel must disclose outside employment, affiliations, and other activities as required by HOP 5-2011.

D. Research Support

Authors should acknowledge sources of support that enabled the work being published. These include financial support such as grants, contracts or gifts; salary support provided by an entity other than the University; technical support; and in-kind support if substantive and important to the completion of the work. Funding sources should be acknowledged when:

1. Providing financial support for research personnel who contributed to the work being reported,
2. Supporting the conduct of experiments or the analysis of data related to the work being reported, or
3. When there is a clear association between the work being reported and the aims and objectives of the funded project.

E. Authorship Disputes

If a difference in scholarly opinion regarding authorship arises, disputing parties are encouraged to consult the University's Responsible Authorship Guidance to resolve the matter through direct resolution. In the event that disputing parties are unable to come to a satisfactory agreement, each party may involve their respective department chair for additional assistance. At any time, disputing parties may consult the appropriate University Ombuds Office to explore additional options for resolution. Authorship disputes that involve a credible and specific allegation of research misconduct as defined in HOP 7-1230, Research Misconduct, should be reported to the University's Research Integrity Officer (RIO).

VIII. Forms & Tools
None

IX. Frequently Asked Questions
None

X. Related Information
Regents' *Rules and Regulations*, Rule 90101 – Intellectual Property
HOP 5-2011 - Conflict of Interest, Conflict of Commitment, and Outside Activities
HOP 7-1210 – Promoting Objectivity in Research by Managing, Reducing or Eliminating Financial Conflicts of Interest
HOP 7-1230 - Research Misconduct
Responsible Authorship Guidance

XI. History
Origination date: October 27, 2022
    Next scheduled review: October 2025

Figure 7.3. *(continued)*

JOURNAL AUTHORSHIP POLICIES

Journal authorship policies will differ somewhat from institutional authorship policies by tailoring them to the authoring and authorship role while institutional policies are geared toward authors-as-employees. But both have similar ends, which is to communicate expectations about whom to include as authors on a shared work of authorship.

NATURE—*EDITORIAL POLICY ON AUTHORSHIP*

Nature has a robust authorship policy. It includes excellent guidance on what activities meet authorship criteria and it also incorporates ethical principles for equity and inclusion both for authorship and for research practices. It also helpfully includes a section on generative artificial intelligence providing clear and accurate terms that such applications do not constitute authorship, but instead serve as a significant data source requiring acknowledgment.

Editorial policies

Authorship

Competing interests

Research Ethics

Reporting standards and
availability of data, materials,
code and protocols

Image integrity and standards

Plagiarism and duplicate
publication

Corrections, Retractions and
Matters Arising

Peer Review

Confidentiality

Acknowledgements

Preprints & Conference
Proceedings

Press and embargo policies

Self archiving and license to
publish

Authorship

On this page

- Authorship
- Authorship: inclusion & ethics in global research
- Consortia authorship
- Author contribution statements
- Author identification
- Author name change
- Nature Portfolio journals' editorials

Authorship

Authorship provides credit for a researcher's contributions to a study and carries accountability. Authors are expected to fulfil the criteria below (adapted from McNutt et al., Proceedings of the National Academy of Sciences, Feb 2018, 201715374; DOI: 10.1073/pnas.1715374115; licensed under CC BY 4.0):

Each author is expected to have made substantial contributions to the conception or design of the work; or the acquisition, analysis, or interpretation of data; or the creation of new software used in the work; or have drafted the work or substantively revised it

AND to have approved the submitted version (and any substantially modified version that involves the author's contribution to the study);

(continued)

Figure 7.4. *Nature* Editorial Policy on Authorship

AND to have agreed both to be personally accountable for the author's own contributions and to ensure that questions related to the accuracy or integrity of any part of the work, even ones in which the author was not personally involved, are appropriately investigated, resolved, and the resolution documented in the literature.

Nature Portfolio journals encourage collaboration with colleagues in the locations where the research is conducted, and expect their inclusion as co-authors when they fulfil all authorship criteria described above. Contributors who do not meet all criteria for authorship should be listed in the Acknowledgements section.

Large Language Models (LLMs), such as ChatGPT, do not currently satisfy our authorship criteria. Notably an attribution of authorship carries with it accountability for the work, which cannot be effectively applied to LLMs. Use of an LLM should be properly documented in the Methods section (and if a Methods section is not available, in a suitable alternative part) of the manuscript.

Nature Portfolio journals reserve the right not to consider non-primary research manuscripts that have been authored by medical writers. Writing assistance should be acknowledged in all article types.

Nature Portfolio journals do not require all authors of a research paper to sign the letter of submission, nor do they impose an order on the list of authors. Submission to a Nature Portfolio journal is taken by the journal to mean that all the listed authors have agreed all of the contents, including the author list and author contribution statements. The corresponding author is responsible for having ensured that this agreement has been reached that all authors have agreed to be so listed, and have approved the manuscript submission to the journal, and for managing all communication between the journal and all co-authors, before and after publication. The corresponding author is also responsible for submitting a competing interests' statement on behalf of all authors of the paper; please refer to our competing interests' policy for more information.

It is expected that the corresponding author (and on multi-group collaborations, at least one member of each collaborating group, usually the most senior member of each submitting group or team, who accepts responsibility for the contributions to the manuscript from that team) will be responsible for the following with respect to data, code and materials: (adapted from McNutt et al., Proceedings of the National Academy of Sciences, Feb 2018, 201715374; DOI: 10.1073/pnas.1715374115; licensed under CC BY 4.0):

- ensuring that data, materials, and code comply with transparency and reproducibility standards of the field and journal;
- ensuring that original data/materials/code upon which the submission is based are preserved following best practices in the field so that they are retrievable for reanalysis;
- confirming that data/materials/code presentation accurately reflects the original;
- foreseeing and minimizing obstacles to the sharing of data/materials/code described in the work
- ensuring that all authors (or group leaders in multi-lab collaborations) have certified the author list and author contributions

Figure 7.4. *(continued)*

At submission, the corresponding author must include written permission from the authors of the work concerned for mention of any unpublished material cited in the manuscript (for example others' data, in press manuscripts, personal communications or work in preparation). The corresponding author also must clearly identify at submission any material within the manuscript (such as figures) that has been published previously elsewhere and provide written permission from authors of the prior work and/or publishers, as appropriate, for the re-use of such material.

After acceptance, the corresponding author is responsible for the accuracy of all content in the proof, including the names of co-authors, addresses and affiliations.

After publication, the corresponding author is the point of contact for queries about the published paper. It is their responsibility to inform all co-authors of any matters arising in relation to the published paper and to ensure such matters are dealt with promptly. Authors of published material have a responsibility to inform the journal immediately if they become aware of any aspects that requires correction.

Any changes to the author list after submission, such as a change in the order of the authors or the deletion or addition of authors, must be approved by every author. Nature Portfolio journal editors are not in a position to investigate or adjudicate authorship disputes before or after publication. Such disagreements, if they cannot be resolved amongst authors, should be directed to the relevant institutional authority.

The primary affiliation for each author should be the institution where the majority of their work was done. If an author has subsequently moved, the current address may also be stated. Springer Nature remains neutral with regard to jurisdictional claims in published maps and institutional affiliations.

Top of page ⇧

Authorship: inclusion & ethics in global research

Nature Portfolio journals encourage collaboration with colleagues in the locations where the research is conducted, and expect their inclusion as co-authors when they fulfill all authorship criteria described above. Contributors who do not meet all criteria for authorship should be listed in the Acknowledgements section. We urge researchers to carefully consider researcher contributions and authorship criteria when involved in multi-region collaborations involving local researchers so as to promote greater equity in research collaborations.

We encourage researchers to follow the recommendations set out in the Global Code of Conduct for Research in Resource-Poor Settings when designing, executing and reporting their research and to provide a disclosure statement in their manuscript that covers the aspects listed below (drawn from the Global Code of Conduct) Editors may at their discretion ask authors to provide a disclosure statement taking these questions into account; the disclosure can be requested during peer review, shared with reviewers and published in the final paper as an "Ethics & Inclusion statement" in the Methods section. Our general policies on Research ethics and Reporting standards can be found here and here.

(continued)

Figure 7.4. *(continued)*

1. Has the research included local researchers throughout the research process – study design, study implementation, data ownership, intellectual property and authorship of publications?

2. Is the research locally relevant and has this been determined in collaboration with local partners?

3. Please describe whether roles and responsibilities were agreed amongst collaborators ahead of the research and whether any capacity-building plans for local researchers were discussed.

4. Would this research have been severely restricted or prohibited in the setting of the researchers? If yes, please provide details on specific exceptions granted for this research in agreement with local stakeholders.

5. Where appropriate, has the study been approved by a local ethics review committee? If not, please explain the reasons.

6. Where animal welfare regulations, environmental protection and biorisk-related regulations in the local research setting were insufficient compared to the setting of the researchers, please describe if research was undertaken to the higher standards.

7. Does the research result in stigmatization, incrimination, discrimination or otherwise personal risk to participants? If yes, describe provisions to ensure safety and well-being of participants.

8. If research involves health, safety, security or other risk to researchers, describe any risk management plans undertaken.

9. Have any benefit sharing measures been discussed in case biological materials, cultural artefacts or associated traditional knowledge has been transferred out of the country?

10. Please indicate if you have taken local and regional research relevant to your study into account in citations.

Consortia authorship

A collective of authors can be listed as a consortium. If necessary, individual authors can be listed in both the main author list and as a member of a consortium. All authors within a consortium must be listed at the end of the paper. If it is necessary to include a list of consortium members that did not directly contribute to the paper, this list can be placed in the Supplementary Information. To facilitate submission of manuscripts with large author lists, please consult the journal editor before submission.

Top of page ↑

Author contribution statements

Nature Portfolio journals encourage transparency by publishing author contribution statements. Authors are required to include a statement of responsibility in the manuscript, including review-type articles, that specifies the contribution of every author. The level of detail varies; some disciplines produce manuscripts that comprise discrete efforts readily articulated in detail, whereas other fields operate as group efforts at all stages. Author contribution statements are included in the published paper. This Nature Editorial describes the policy in more detail.

Figure 7.4. *(continued)*

Nature Portfolio journals also allow one set of co-authors to be specified as having contributed equally to the work and one set of co-authors to be specified as having jointly supervised the work. Other equal contributions are best described in author contribution statements. Corresponding authors have specific responsibilities (described above).

Top of page ↑

Author identification

As part of our efforts to improve transparency and unambiguous attribution of scholarly contributions, corresponding authors of published papers must provide their Open Researcher and Contributor Identifier (ORCID) iD; co-authors are encouraged to provide ORCiD iDs. More information about Springer Nature's support for ORCiD iDs and journals participating in the ORCiD mandate can be found here.

Top of page ↑

Author name change

An author who has changed their name for reasons such as gender transition or religious conversion may request for their name, pronouns and other relevant biographical information to be corrected on papers published prior to the change. The author can choose for this correction to happen silently, in which case there will be no note flagging the change on either the pdf or the html of the paper, or alternatively they may do so by a formal public Author Correction.

Top of page ↑

Nature Portfolio journals' editorials:

- New framework aims to improve inclusion and ethics in global research collaborations amid wider efforts to end exploitative practices. *Nature. Nature addresses helicopter research and ethics dumping,* June 2022.
- Corresponding authors should not neglect their responsibility to a journal or their co-authors. *Nature Nanotechnology.* A matter of duty, December 2012.
- Why do we need statements to define the contributions made by each author? *Nature Photonics.* Contributors, guests, and ghosts, June 2012.
- Announcing "author contributions" statements, 2009:
  - *Nature Nanotechnology.* The responsibilities of authors.
  - *Nature Cell Biology.* Attribution and accountability.
  - *Nature Physics.* What did you do?
  - *Nature Photonics.* Combating plagiarism.
  - *Nature.* Authorship policies.

- Individual contributions should be carefully evaluated when compiling the author list of a scientific paper. *Nature Materials.* Authorship matters, February 2008.
- How the responsibilities of co-authors for a scientific paper's integrity could be made more explicit. *Nature.* Who is accountable? 1 November 2007.
- The problems of unjustified authorship. *Nature Materials.* Authorship without authorization, November 2004.

Nature is encouraging authors of papers to say who did what. *Nature.* Author contributions, 3 June 1999.

Figure 7.4. *(continued)*

FRONTIERS IN DIGITAL HUMANITIES—EQUAL CONTRIBUTION AUTHOR GUIDELINES

The journal *Frontiers in Digital Humanities* provides useful guidelines on indicating author contribution. This type of journal policy will require that the research group have initial conversations about author order informed by copyright ownership. To adhere to this journal policy, the convener of the research group would establish a local authorship policy or practice. This policy or practice would, in turn, be informed by the convener's institutional copyright ownership and authorship policies.

Equal contributions

The authors who have contributed equally should be marked with a symbol (†) in the author list of the doc/latex and pdf files of the manuscript uploaded at submission.

Please use the appropriate standard statement(s) to indicate equal contributions:

- **Equal contribution:** These authors contributed equally to this work
- **First authorship:** These authors share first authorship
- **Senior authorship:** These authors share senior authorship
- **Last authorship:** These authors share last authorship
- **Equal contribution and first authorship:** These authors contributed equally to this work and share first authorship
- **Equal contribution and senior authorship:** These authors contributed equally to this work and share senior authorship
- **Equal contribution and last authorship:** These authors contributed equally to this work and share last authorship

Example: Max Maximus 1†, John Smith2† and Barbara Smith1 †These authors contributed equally to this work and share first authorship

Figure 7.5. *Frontiers in Digital Humanities* Equal Contribution Guidelines

PUBLISHER AUTHORSHIP POLICIES

Publishers' authorship policies will be different from institutional and journal policies because they will apply to several (or all) of a publishers' scholarly communication venues, including journals, conferences, and potentially books. Like journal policies, they will be written for authors of all types as a way to establish expectations about the relationship between the publisher and the corresponding author. Most will incorporate guidelines developed by the Committee on Publication Ethics, a non-profit based in the United Kingdom (publicationethics.org).

ASSOCIATION FOR COMPUTING MACHINERY POLICY ON AUTHORSHIP

The Association for Computing Machinery (ACM) provides an excellent example of a publisher authorship policy. It specifies guidance on authorship criteria and asks that authors appropriately acknowledge the contributions of others. This will require that convening authors, again, have a local policy or practice on authorship based on institutional copyright ownership and authorship policies. It helpfully provides a listing of what authors can expect from ACM as a publisher and asks that all of the association's scholarly communication venues point to the policy for consistent application.

ACM Policy on Authorship

Approved by the ACM Publications Board on April 20, 2023

Introduction

The computing community expects ACM Publications to adhere to the highest standards for quality and trustworthiness and for ACM authors to engage in ethical practices while conducting research and reporting on the results of that research in ACM Publications. The community also expects ACM authors to respect the intellectual property rights of others by providing proper credit to all those contributing to the published Work and to give proper attribution to all those whose work is included in any new Work published by ACM. Likewise, the community expects ACM and its volunteers to provide the highest quality of service throughout the publication process, including an ethical process for managing submissions and peer review, free from bias, collusion, plagiarism, deception and other forms of misconduct that erode trust in ACM Publications and in science more generally.

To ensure that ACM's Policy on Authorship is consistent with best practices and international publishing standards, ACM has become an active member of the Committee on Publication Ethics (COPE) ↗ and is committed to ensuring that ACM's Policy on Authorship is generally consistent with COPE's definition of authorship, which can be found here ↗. While there are many aspects of COPE's definition of authorship that have influenced ACM's Policy, there are three concepts in particular that impacted ACM's updated Policy, including:

- Authors must be the "creator or originator of an idea" and/or Work
- Authors must make a substantial contribution to the Work
- Authors must be accountable for the work that was done and its presentation in a publication

By updating ACM's Policy on Authorship, it is ACM's goal to provide additional guidance and clarity for what is acceptable publishing practice when publishing with ACM, especially with respect to the rapid technological changes taking place with the introduction of generative AI tools and technologies.

Scope of Policy

This policy applies to all submitted, accepted, and published articles in all ACM Publication venues, including ACM journals, ACM conferences, ICPS conferences, ACM magazines, and ACM books.

ACM journals, magazines, and conferences, and ICPS conferences shall reference this Policy in Calls for Papers, Instructions for Authors, and other solicitations of submissions. The reference to this Policy should appear alongside other venue-specific policies. All of the above publication venues are also encouraged to incorporate acknowledgement of these representations into their respective paper submissions process.

Criteria for Authorship

ACM has established a more detailed criteria for determining if an individual's contribution to a Work rises to the level of authorship or if they should be acknowledged for their contribution in the acknowledgements section of a work.

Anyone listed as author on an ACM submission must meet all the following criteria:

- They are an identifiable human being. Anonymous authorship is not permitted, although pseudonyms and/or pen names are permitted provided accurate contact information is given to ACM. ACM does not currently permit collective authorship.
- They have made substantial intellectual contributions to some components of the original Work described in the manuscript, such as contributing to the conception, design, and analysis of the study reported on in the Work and participating in the drafting and/or revision of the manuscript.
- They take full responsibility for all content in the published Works.

Note: All individuals who meet the above criteria should be listed as authors on the Work. The practices of gift authorship, guest authorship, ghost authorship* (see the FAQ for detailed definitions of these and related terms and for discussion of related, acceptable practices), and purchased authorship are clear violations of ACM Publications Policy and whose proven may have severe consequences for those found to have participated in such practices. For more information about these practices, please see the FAQ document.

In addition, all persons listed as an author on an ACM submission certify that:

- They are aware the manuscript has been submitted for publication to ACM.
- They agree to be held responsible and accountable for any issues relating to the correctness or integrity of the Work and compliance with all related ACM Publications Policies with the understanding that, depending on the circumstances, not all authors will necessarily be held equally accountable.
- That the Work submitted is original, that the listed authors are the creators of the Work, that each author is aware of the submission and that they are listed as an author, and that the paper is an honest representation of the underlying Work.

ACM Case Studies ↗

Written by leading domain experts for software engineers, ACM Case Studies provide an in-depth look at how software teams overcome specific challenges by implementing new technologies, adopting new practices, or a combination of both. Often through first-hand accounts, these pieces explore what the challenges were, the tools and techniques that were used to combat them, and the solution that was achieved.

CAREER RESOURCE
Lifelong Learning ↗

ACM offers lifelong learning resources including online books and courses from Skillsoft, TechTalks on the hottest topics in computing and IT, and more.

PUBLISH YOUR WORK
Publish with ACM

ACM's prestigious conferences and journals seek top-quality papers in all areas of computing and IT. It is now easier than ever to find the most appropriate venue for your research and publish with ACM.

(continued)

Figure 7.6. Association for Computing Machinery Policy on Authorship

- They will provide ACM with a valid ORCID prior to completion of the ACM eRights process (an ORCID is a unique author ID that can be obtained from www.orcid.org). This is required for author identification purposes and to improve the normalization of publishing-related data in the ACM Digital Library.

Authors who meet the above authorship criteria, but who die or become incapacitated prior to publication can be listed as co-authors with permission of their estate or next of kin.

Those who contributed to a Work, but whose contribution does not rise to the level of authorship, may be acknowledged at the end of the Work, before the Bibliography, with explicitly described roles, preferably using the roles found in the CRediT (Contributor Roles Taxonomy). In addition, those whose contribution does rise to the level of authorship, but who are unable to publish with ACM as a result of active publication bans may be acknowledged in the acknowledgment section of the Work.

Generative AI tools and technologies, such as ChatGPT, may not be listed as authors of an ACM published Work. The use of generative AI tools and technologies to create content is permitted but must be fully disclosed in the Work. For example, the authors could include the following statement in the Acknowledgements section of the Work: ChatGPT was utilized to generate sections of this Work, including text, tables, graphs, code, data, citations, etc.). If you are uncertain about the need to disclose the use of a particular tool, err on the side of caution, and include a disclosure in the acknowledgements section of the Work.

Basic word processing systems that recommend and insert replacement text, perform spelling or grammar checks and corrections, or systems that do language translations are to be considered exceptions to this disclosure requirement and are generally permitted and need not be disclosed in the Work. As the line between Generative AI tools and basic word processing systems like MS-Word or Grammarly becomes blurred, this Policy will be updated.

Criteria for Submission

All ACM submissions shall meet the following requirements:

- That the Work submitted is not currently under review at any other publication venue, and that it will not be submitted to another publication venue unless it has been rejected or withdrawn from this venue. There may be exceptions to this requirement for certain conference Works, including submission to a non-publishing venue, such as a workshop, where the Work will not be formally published. If the author is requesting an exception, they should contact the Program Chair of the ACM conference. Posting a pre-print version of the Work to arXiv or a similar pre-print venue is not considered a prior or current publication venue and there is no need to request an exception for such postings.
- That all authors have the right and intent to publish the Work in the venue to which it is submitted if the work is accepted. For conference papers, this includes the expected ability and intent to have an author of the paper register for and attend the conference to present the paper, if required. Please refer to the specific policies of individual conferences for registration and presentation requirements for named authors, including the ability to present virtually or in person. Many conferences have changed their specific requirements as a result of the recent COVID-19 pandemic.
- That any prior publications on which this Work is based are documented appropriately in the Work. This documentation includes providing an explanation of the incremental contribution of a journal paper that extends prior results published in a conference paper. (In cases of double- anonymous review, this information should be supplied to the editor or program chair only.)

In addition to the above requirements, all ACM authors shall be required to comply with all other ACM Publications Policies detailed in individual Calls for Papers and Instructions for authors of individual ACM Publications, including journals, conferences, books, newsletters, etc.

Frequently Asked Questions

Please find a list of frequently asked questions and answers related to ACM's updated Policy on Authorship here.

Related ACM Policies

Conference of Publication Policy ⌐
Policy on Plagiarism, Misrepresentation, and Falsification ⌐
Conflict of Interest Policy ⌐
Inappropriate Content Policy ⌐
Policy on Peer Review ⌐
Policy on Research Involving Human Participants and Subjects ⌐
Policy on Submitting and Investigating Claims ⌐
Confidentiality Policy ⌐
Policy on Communicating Results of Investigations ⌐
Appealing Policy Violation Decisions ⌐
Penalties for Publication Violations ⌐

External Resources

ACM is an active member of the Committee on Publication Ethics (COPE) ⌐. COPE provides guidance and standards of practice for publishers and the scientific community, as well as educational resources that will help ACM authors to follow aceptable publishing practice. The following documents should be referenced in connection with ACM's Authorship Policy:

- https://publicationethics.org/sites/default/files/COPE_DD_A4_Authorship_SEPT19_SCREEN_AW.pdf ⌐
- https://publicationethics.org/resources/seminars-and-webinars/ethical-versus-fraudulent-authorship ⌐

Contact ACM

The ACM Director of Publications should be contacted for any:

- Questions about the interpretation of this policy
- Questions about appealing violation decisions
- Requests for deviations from, or extensions to, this policy
- Reporting of egregious behavior related to this policy, including purposeful evasion of the policy, false reporting, or coercion

Mailing address:

ACM Director of Publications
Association for Computing Machinery
1601 Broadway, 10th Floor
New York, NY 10019-7434
Phone: +1-212-626-0659

Or via email:

scott.delman@hq.acm.org

Figure 7.6. *(continued)*

TAYLOR & FRANCIS—EDITORIAL POLICIES ON AUTHORSHIP

Taylor & Francis has a comprehensive policy on authorship that applies to all of its journals (it does not indicate if it also applies to books and conferences) and also addresses the use of generative artificial intelligence. It takes the approach from the role of corresponding author, which essentially will require that research managers again initiate conversations in advance about authorship practices. The research convener would follow an institutional copyright ownership policy and obtain guidance on authorship practices through an institutional authorship policy.

Taylor & Francis Editorial Policies on Authorship

The following instructions (part of our Editorial Policies ⧉) apply to all Taylor & Francis Group journals.

Corresponding author

Co-authors must agree on who will take on the role of corresponding author. It is then the responsibility of the corresponding author to reach consensus with all co-authors regarding all aspects of the article, prior to submission. This includes the authorship list and order, and list of correct affiliations.

The corresponding author is also responsible for liaising with co-authors regarding any editorial queries. And, they act on behalf of all co-authors in any communication about the article throughout: submission, peer review, production, and after publication. The corresponding author signs the publishing agreement on behalf of all the listed authors.

AI-based tools and technologies for content generation

Authors must be aware that using AI-based tools and technologies for article content generation, e.g. large language models (LLMs), generative AI, and chatbots (e.g. ChatGPT), is not in line with our authorship criteria.

All authors are wholly responsible for the originality, validity and integrity of the content of their submissions. Therefore, LLMs and other similar types of tools do not meet the criteria for authorship.

Changes in authorship

Any changes in authorship prior to or after publication must be agreed upon by all authors - including those authors being added or removed. It is the responsibility of the corresponding author to obtain confirmation from all co-authors and to provide a completed Authorship Change Request form ⧉ to the editorial office.

If a change in authorship is necessary after publication, this will be amended via a post-publication notice. Any changes in authorship must comply with our criteria for authorship. And requests for significant changes to the authorship list, after the article has been accepted, may be rejected if clear reasons and evidence of author contributions cannot be provided.

Assistance from scientific, medical, technical writers or translators

Contributions made by professional scientific, medical or technical writers, translators or anyone who has assisted with the manuscript content, must be acknowledged. Their source of funding must also be declared.

They should be included in an 'Acknowledgments' section with an explanation of their role, or they should be included in the author list if appropriate.

Authors are advised to consult the joint position statement ⧉ from American Medical Writers Association (AMWA), European Medical Writers Association (EMWA), and International Society of Medical Publication Professionals (ISMPP).

Assistance with experiments and data analysis

Any significant contribution to the research reported, should be appropriately credited according to our authorship criteria.

If any parts of the research were outsourced to professional laboratories or to data analysts, this should be clearly stated within the manuscript, alongside an explanation of their role. Or, they should be included in the author list if appropriate.

Authors are responsible for retaining all of the original data related to their work, and should be prepared to share it with the journal editorial office if requested.

Figure 7.7. Taylor & Francis Editorial Policies on Authorship

This chapter highlighted policies that encourage equitable and inclusive authorship practices. These sample policies can be drawn upon by research administrators, authors, editors, and publishers to establish local policies that reflect similar principles applicable to their area's respective activities. Building upon the concepts reflected in earlier chapters, all of those involved in the scholarly communication system can utilize the components of this chapter to establish policies and practices that ensure a diverse, equitable, and inclusive community for academic authors.

Resources and Further Reading

This book provided best practices on how to develop copyright ownership and authorship policies by reviewing the concepts of authorship, copyright basics, and ways of incorporating policy elements to achieve equitable and inclusive authorship plans for research teams and projects. For additional resources on establishing diverse research teams, please see:

BOOKS ABOUT DIVERSE TEAMS

The Business of Race: How to Create and Sustain an Antiracist Workplace—And Why It's Actually Good for Business by Margaret H. Greenberg and Gina Greenlee

Hiring for Diversity: The Guide to Building an Inclusive and Equitable Organization by Arthur Woods and Susanna Tharakan

Perspectives on Gender and Work by Eden B. King, Quinetta M. Roberson, and Mikki R. Hebl

The Elephant and the Mouse: Moving Beyond the Illusion of Inclusion to Create a Truly Diverse and Equitable Workplace by Laura A. Liswood

WEBSITES ABOUT DIVERSE TEAMS AND POLICY WRITING

DIY Committee Guide https://www.diycommitteeguide.org
ePolicy Institute http://www.epolicyinstitute.com
Policy Writing Tips https://www.mtu.edu/policy/tips/
Project Include https://projectinclude.org

BOOKS ABOUT COPYRIGHT

Law and Authors: A Legal Handbook for Writers by Jacqueline D. Lipton

Getting Permission: How to License & Clear Copyrighted Materials Online & Off by Richard Stim

The Copyright Book: A Practical Guide by William S. Strong

The Public Domain: How to Find & Use Copyright-Free Writings, Music, Art & More by Attorney Stephen Fishman

WEBSITES ABOUT COPYRIGHT AND AUTHORSHIP

U.S. Copyright Office https://www.copyright.gov
American Library Association Copyright Tools http://www.ala.org/advocacy
   /copyright-tools
National Writers Union https://nwu.org/
Authors Guild https://authorsguild.org/

Index

About the Author

Allyson Mower, MA, MLIS is the author of *Copyright Policies & Workflows in Libraries: A Concise Handbook* and the librarian for scholarly communication and copyright at the University of Utah Marriott Library. She studies authorship, reading, and publishing in addition to current practices of copyright in libraries. She researched, presented on, and wrote "The University of Utah, Its Authors, and Their Works, 1883–1970," a descriptive bibliography (https://authors.lib .utah.edu). Allyson also developed a theory of academic authorship to inform an authorship policy at the University of Utah and assisted in its implementation in 2021. In addition to being the scholarly communication and copyright librarian, Allyson also currently serves as the policy liaison for the University of Utah Academic Senate helping to get new policies reviewed and approved by faculty, students, and administrators. She lives in Salt Lake City with her spouse.

www.ingramcontent.com/pod-product-compliance
Lightning Source LLC
Chambersburg PA
CBHW061609220326
41598CB00024BC/3510